DEFINING MOMENTS

WORLD
WAR II

DEFINING MOMENTS
WORLD
WAR II

Alex Hook

THUNDER BAY
P·R·E·S·S

San Diego, California

THUNDER BAY
P · R · E · S · S

Thunder Bay Press
An imprint of the Advantage Publishers Group
5880 Oberlin Drive, San Diego, CA 92121-4794
www.thunderbaybooks.com

Copyright © TAJ Books Ltd, 2005

All notations of errors or omissions should be addressed to Thunder Bay Press,
Editorial Department, at the above address. All other correspondence (author inquiries,
permissions) concerning the content of this book should be addressed to:
TAJ Books, 27 Ferndown Gardens, Cobham, Surrey, UK, KT11 2BH,
info@tajbooks.com.

ISBN 1-59223-434-8

Library of Congress Cataloging-in-Publication Data available upon request.

Printed in China
1 2 3 4 5 09 08 07 06 05

CONTENTS

DECADE	PAGE

Introduction

When wars are examined in detail, it can be seen that they are actually made up of many individual events, such as battles, retreats, victories, and surrenders. Each of these can be further subdivided into the various components from which they are formed—the causes, the participants, the preliminaries, the key stages, and so on. However, when a war lasts for many years, and is spread right around the globe, the story can become very complicated indeed. Sense can be made out of all the seemingly unrelated parts if the key events are distilled out and laid bare for all to see. Such a process has been performed here to create this book. Each of the key moments in World War II has been identified and presented in such a way as to allow the whole picture to be understood from the ground up.

To follow the structure of this book it is first necessary to understand what goes into making up a "key moment." Some events are so obvious that they need little justification—when Hitler invaded Poland or Japan attacked Pearl Harbor, for instance. Others, however, may seem at first sight to be of little overall significance yet some of these then caused other more important events to take place. The Battle of the Barents Sea is a good example—here a small naval conflict took place. In itself, this was nothing unusual but the poor performance of the German navy so outraged Hitler that he nearly had the entire surface fleet broken up for scrap. From this point on, his warships ceased to have any significant impact on the war—much to the surprise and benefit of the Allies.

German troops parade through Warsaw, Poland.

At the time this photo was made, smoke billowed 20,000 feet above Hiroshima while smoke from the burst of the first atomic bomb had spread over 10,000 feet on the target at the base of the rising column. August 5, 1945. Two planes of the 509th Composite Group, part of the 313th Wing of the 20th Air Force, participated in this mission; one to carry the bomb, and the other to act as escort.

There are still other events that mark key moments in history, such as the first time that something important took place. The dropping of the first atomic bomb is perhaps the most significant event of the 20 century, for this single action helped to shape the course of the next 60 years of world politics. For a start, it forced the Japanese to accept an early surrender—something that would have been completely unacceptable to their military commanders in almost any other set of circumstances. The use of the atomic bomb, for all its tragic consequences, may well also have stopped the world sinking into a much deeper conflict. At the time Josef Stalin was about to send his armies to invade Japan, and without the nuclear threat he may well also have continued to move west from Berlin. It is likely that the reign of terror imposed by Adolf Hitler on the people of western Europe would have paled into insignificance had Stalin carried out these plans.

Allied troops land in Normandy, France during Operation "Overlord".

Important decisions can also be considered to be key moments of a war. The decision made by Allied commanders to land invasion forces on the European mainland at Normandy rather than Calais, for instance, was an event of major strategic importance. Likewise, the disastrous decision by Hitler to push for Moscow in the face of the Russian winter and the advice of his Army generals was momentous. Indeed, the decision to attack Russia in itself probably sealed the fate of the Nazi cause from the outset. Had Hitler remained at peace with the Soviets, he may well have had enough men and equipment to inflict far more serious defeats on the West: for example, he could have returned to the invasion of Great Britain. Had this happened successfully, it would have been much harder for the Allies to have staged landings on the European mainland.

In order to understand how and why World War II took the course it followed, it is necessary to understand how all the various theatres interacted. There were basically five different geographical regions—North Africa, western Europe, Russia, the Atlantic, and the Pacific. None of these regions is totally discrete—many overlap, and they all influenced each other. For instance, when large numbers of merchant ships attempting to transport supplies across the Atlantic were sunk by U-boats, both the Russian and African campaigns were affected.

It must also be remembered that the battles were fought on land, sea, and in the air, and so each of these arenas has its own story to tell. In many ways this was a story of differing military cultures. Getting the various armed services to work together as effective combined forces had not been done extensively before, and many painful lessons had to be learned. For instance, many of the American units that landed on the northwest coast of Africa had not seen action before. When they went into battle they continued the regimes that they had used in training camp. This included a command structure that dated back to World War I. All orders were given by senior officers, and then these gradually

Generalfeldmarschall Erwin Rommel, Blue Max and Knights Cross holder, instrumental in the Fall of France 1940, commander of the Afrika Korps and German defences in western Europe.

worked their way down to the front line. In a fast-moving battlefield arena this situation was simply too slow and cumbersome. In the face of the highly experienced Afrika Korps, the Americans fared very badly and experienced heavy losses of both men and equipment.

Fortunately for the troops, the regional commanders quickly realized that a much more responsive command system was needed. Junior officers were therefore duly empowered to make decisions on the ground—this alone made an enormous difference. Further analysis of their humiliating defeats showed that the various force elements were not being used to their full effect. As a result, changes were made so that well co-ordinated troop, artillery, and air force units could be brought to bear on the enemy. The next time Rommel ran up against the Americans, the roles were reversed. He had previously considered them to be ill-disciplined and poorly trained, and that their equipment was second-rate. When his troops were heavily defeated in a straight battle, he was truly shocked.

LSM-151 was part of a US Naval Force assisting the Australian Army during the landing.

In stark contrast, the different Australian forces worked very well together. Their invasion of Borneo—which was excellently planned and implemented— showed how powerful a very close integration of naval, ground, and air units could be. As a result they experienced minimal losses of men and materials, and quickly gained ground against the enemy.

Participation in significant strategic events was not just the preserve of the military. Civilian populations also played their part. The most impressive display of "people power" was effected in the early stages of the war when Axis armies were advancing toward Moscow. The Soviets quickly realized that the enemy was likely to capture most of their industrial areas in the western parts of Russia. Since these represented almost the entire country's production capability, Stalin ordered all the factories to be dismantled and moved to safety behind the Ural mountains. In a massed re-location effort—the likes of which had never been seen before (or since)—the people set to, and in an incredible feat of logistics the task was achieved with remarkable alacrity. The entire manufacturing capacity of the Soviet Union was then turned over to war production, and before long heavy equipment such as tanks and aircraft was rolling off the lines in great numbers. This played a critical role in the Soviet Union's ability to go on the offensive and push the Germans all the way back across eastern Europe and right into Berlin itself.

The crew of the B-17 Flying Fortress "Memphis Belle" is shown at an air base in England after completing 25 missions over enemy territory on June 7, 1943.

German soldiers engage in city fighting during operatioon "Barbarossa".

It is also worth noting that while some important events gain notoriety, others seem to sink into obscurity. One of the most compelling tales of bravery and courage in the face of overwhelming odds concerns the Battle of Habbaniya. This almost forgotten conflict was considered by Churchill to be the second most important battle of World War II, after El Alamein. Situated on the River Euphrates, Habbaniya airfield was a backwater training camp used by the British. The battle began in the late spring of 1941, and took place because the Germans wanted to use Iraqi airfields to attack the Middle East. Had they managed this, they would almost certainly have been able to capture the area's oilfields. This would have been a disaster for the Allies, who relied heavily on Arabian wells for their own fuel supplies. It would also have meant the Nazi regime had a second major source of oil, which would have made it far less dependant on the oilfields of the Caucasus region. In the end these proved to be the Reich's Achilles heel—when Soviet forces captured the oil wells of Romania, Hitler's war machine quickly ground to a halt.

In order to prepare for this new offensive in Iraq, the Germans set about instigating an uprising amongst the local population. On May 29, 1941, a large contingent of around 9,000 men and 50 field guns surrounded the Habbaniya airfield. They then proceeded to shell the airbase and shoot at any

aircraft attempting to take off. After an epic struggle of heroic proportions, the small force of defending British officers and men managed to fight off the vastly superior numbers of Iraqi attackers. Even though they had only a few antiquated cadet training aircraft, their crews managed to drop enough bombs to force their attackers to withdraw. Since the aircraft were not equipped with the necessary release racks, the crews often simply pushed bombs out through side hatches with their feet. Had the Germans been able to reinforce the Iraqi forces with even a small contingent of troops, it is unlikely that the British would have been able to hold them off. Although the Germans did finally send some modern bombers, it was a case of too little, too late. This massive blunder was probably caused by Hitler's preoccupation with the launch of Operation "Barbarossa"—the invasion of Russia.

Ordering the defining moments in a chronological sequence makes it possible to see how quickly both Germany and Japan were able to invade large areas in a very short time. It also highlights how long it took for the Allies to re-take the lands that were originally captured in a matter of days. Examination of the detail shows that having superior intelligence was a key tool in the arsenal the Allies used to defeat their enemies. Foremost in this fight were the outstanding abilities of Allied code-breakers, without which the course of the war would certainly have been very different. Perhaps the message here is that, at the end of the day, intellect is more powerful than the gun.

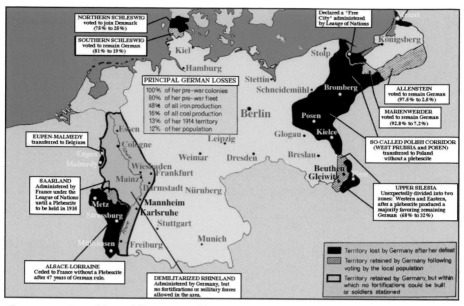

German territorial losses following World War I.

The Treaty of Versailles was the peace settlement which laid out the terms of the punishments imposed on Germany by the Allies for starting World War I. It is thought that somewhere close to 8.5 million people were killed in the war, and around a further 21 million were wounded. The damage caused to vast parts of northeastern Europe was considerable. Massive areas of Belgium had been flattened, and as many as 750,000 French homes were destroyed, along with most of the countries' industrial facilities, such as coal mines. To make matters worse, there were few remaining roads, bridges or telegraph lines—this meant that almost all the infrastructure of the area had to be rebuilt before any significant commerce could take place.

There were many different perspectives on how Germany should be treated. America wanted Europe to sort its own problems out in a way that would lead to a long-term peace, whereas France was primarily interested in making Germany completely powerless. The British also had their own agenda—the rise of Communism in Russia was considered to be a major threat, and allowing Germany to fall victim to it would have been a catastrophe. Lloyd George therefore made harsh noises in public, but behind closed doors ensured that Germany would be left strong enough to resist the red tide.

The treaty ensured that Germany lost a considerable part of her territories to neighboring countries, including vital industrial areas. Her armies were reduced to 100,000 men, and were not allowed tanks, an air force or submarines. The Rhineland was also demilitarized, and there would be an Allied army of occupation for 15 years. Germany had to admit responsibility for starting the war and had to pay for all of the damage. The figure was set at £6,600 million, which was well beyond what Germany was able to pay. The League of Nations was created to keep world peace.

The four Allied leaders during the peace conference (left to right: Georges Clemenceau, French Prime Minister; Woodrow Wilson, U.S. President; Vittorio Orlando (partly hidden), Italian Prime Minister; David Lloyd George, British Prime Minister).

French soldiers waiting in front of the Versailles castle for the signature of the Treaty of Versailles.

Date: .... June 28, 1919
Participants: .... The most important politicians present were:
David Lloyd George of Britain
Georges Clemenceau of France
Woodrow Wilson of America
Location of event: ...... The Hall of Mirrors at the Palace of Versailles, France
Outcome: .... Germany lost large territories to neighboring countries and had to pay for all the war damage. Her armies were also reduced

Hitler and Hindenberg during the opening of the Reichstag March 21st 1933.

JANUARY 30, 1933

By April 1932, the Nazis had so much popular support in Germany that Hitler only just lost out to Hindenburg in the presidential elections. A further round of national elections were held in July, during which the Nazis doubled their representation in the Reichstag, greatly improving their political influence. The large number of Communist representatives meant that it was not possible for the government to form a constructive coalition, so a further national election was held in November 1932. The results were inconclusive, and Hitler quickly exploited the situation, managing to convince many prominent industrialists that a Communist revolution was underway. They in turn put Hindenburg under pressure, and on January 30, 1933, he caved in and made Hitler Chancellor of Germany. Hindenburg had thought that he could control Hitler, but events soon proved him wrong.

Hitler started a media campaign almost immediately—this was aimed at promoting the Nazis as a party, and was organized by his master manipulator, Joseph Goebbels. Giving a blanket coverage of the Nazis'

main policies, it was aimed at the disaffected unemployed, as well as the large numbers of people whose standard of living had declined since the end of World War I.

Hitler then began to remove any sign of opposition from his potential enemies. The Nazis had a word which described how they intended to go about this Gleichschaltung (which translates as "consolidation" or "synchronization"). In effect, this was the establishment of a system that controlled and co-ordinated all aspects of society. The starting point was the elimination of any non-Nazi organizations that could exert influence over the people—these included trade unions and political parties. Even the church did not escape this process, and the Nazis soon totally dominated the political scene.

Date:........................January 30, 1933
Participants: ....Hindenburg, Adolf Hitler and the Nazi Party
Location of event:......Germany
Outcome: ....Hitler became Chancellor of Germany

Spanish refugees in France.

JULY 18, 1936–MARCH 28, 1939

The Spanish Civil War was effectively the opening round of World War II. The principal cause was instability brought on by desperate and widespread poverty. The right-wing military considered itself the only defense against wholesale civil disorder, and when a left-wing Popular Front government was elected in 1936 matters came to a head. The fears of rich landowners and industrialists were exploited by senior army officers who planned a military coup. The rebellion started on July 18, 1936, and although the instigators expected a rapid victory, they instead met with fierce resistance from a determined populace. In order to avoid defeat, they appealed to the military dictatorships of Italy, Germany and Portugal for help. Before long they had support in the form of men and supplies from all three countries.

One of the main problems facing the military was that a large part of their forces were stranded in Morocco with no method of getting back to the Spanish mainland. Known as "The Army of Africa," they were under the command of General Francisco Franco. Without their support, the military would have been in serious trouble—it was at this point that

General Francisco Franco.

Hitler and Mussolini came to the rescue with the provision of enough transport aircraft to move them to Seville. The Nazis took a much more sinister part in the war when, on April 26, 1937, Hitler's Condor Legion firebombed the Basque town of Guernica and reduced it to ruins. By the time of the campaign of March 1938, the Italians and Germans had provided over 600 warplanes to aid the Spanish Fascists. Meanwhile, the governments of the rest of the world stood by and watched, even after Germany invaded Austria. When the Munich Accord was signed, all hope of international assistance came to an end. In late November 1938, Hitler resupplied the Fascists with more weapons; Franco then began his final offensive. After taking Barcelona and the fall of Madrid, the Spanish Civil War officially came to an end on April 1, 1939.

Date:.........................July 18, 1936–March 28, 1939
Participants: ....Fascist and left-wing armies
Location of event:......Spain
Outcome: ....The Fascist regime under General Francisco Franco took
                     power in Spain

Rare photograph of Japan's assault on Shanghai in the early days of the Japanese invasion of China, ca. fall of 1937.

JULY 7, 1937

Japan's invasion of China in 1937 was made possible because the country had been in more or less total disarray since it had been declared a republic on October 10, 1911. Many areas were dominated by ruthless warlords who were more interested in fighting each other than taking on any invading armies. The Japanese had already taken neighboring Manchuria in 1931, and so were well aware of the internal problems that China was experiencing. When they finally attacked on July 7, 1937, they soon occupied both Peking and Shanghai. They continued to make territorial gains, and by December they had taken Nanking, which was full of civilian refugees. A torrent of atrocities was then exacted on the helpless occupants, and many hundreds of thousands died at the hands of the invading Japanese soldiers.

By the time that war started in Europe there had been more than 2 million Chinese casualties, and the country was racked with disease and famine. The Allies tried to support the Chinese with supplies along the 700-mile-long Burma Road but corruption and internal fighting meant that much of this effort was wasted. The road was soon lost to

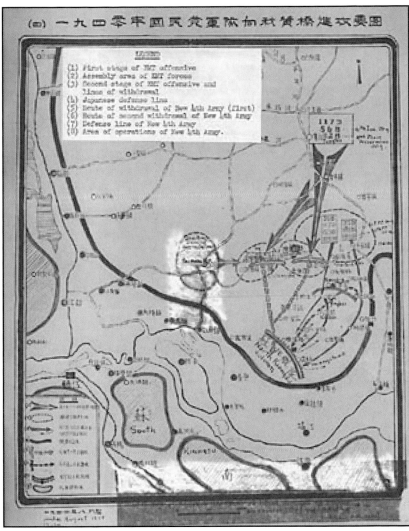

Map showing stages of military confrontation between Communist and Nationalist troops, 1939-1941.

advancing Japanese forces, and Allied support had to be flown in over the Himalayas, which was very dangerous for the Western aircrews involved.

The Allies initially wanted to regain Chinese lands so that they could establish airfields that would be within range of the Japanese mainland. It soon became clear, however, that political problems would prevent this from being a realistic aim—instead, the Allies decided to embark on their campaign to retake the Pacific islands.

Date:........................July 7, 1937
Participants: ....Japanese and Chinese armies—some of the latter under the command of Chiang Kai-shek
Location of event:......Peking and Shanghai
Outcome: ....Much of China fell into Japanese hands

Nazi rally, prior to the invasion of the Rhineland.

MARCH 7, 1936–MARCH 16, 1939

March 7, 1936—German troops occupy the Rhineland

On March 7, 1936, Hitler ordered his troops to re-occupy the Rhineland. This was strictly against the terms of the Versailles and Locarno Treaties, in which the Germans agreed to comply with the demilitarization of the zone. Hitler knew that the Allies wanted to avoid going to war, but he also knew that his forces were not strong enough to fight them. In March 1936, he followed his instincts, and sent his troops in to the Rhineland; in order to stave off any reprisals from the Allies, Hitler offered non-aggression pacts to France and Belgium, and even said that Germany would rejoin the League of Nations. To his great relief, the Allies merely made verbal condemnations, and did nothing more.

March 12-13, 1938—Germany announces Anschluss (union) with Austria

When Germany annexed Austria in spring 1938, the Nazis began systematically expelling the large numbers of Jews from the country. Although the rich could afford to pay for travel to friendlier shores, the poorer elements could not. In order to organize their expulsion, the Nazis set up the "Central Office of Jewish Emigration" in Vienna. This was overseen by Adolf Eichmann, who ran the system there very smoothly and efficiently—he was known to his peers as the "Jewish Specialist." He extorted large sums of money from the richer members of the Jewish community to pay for exit visas for the poor. Within 18 months, he had reduced the Jewish population in Austria by half.

October 15, 1938—German troops occupy the Sudetenland and the Czech government resigns

Hitler knew that Britain and France were unlikely to go to war over territorial demands for parts of Czechoslovakia. However, he was conscious that if those countries allied with the Soviet Union, Germany would be at risk. A conference was held in Munich where representatives from Germany, Britain, France and Italy discussed the current situation. Hitler managed to allay fears of further territorial expansion by promising that this would be the last demand he would make. Both Britain and France were desperate to avoid war, and used Hitler's promises of future non-aggression as an excuse to hand over the Sudetenland. The transferral, which became known as the Munich Agreement, infuriated the Czechs, but they were bluntly told that Britain would not go to war over the Sudetenland.

March 15-16, 1939—Nazis take Czechoslovakia

This act of appeasement over the Sudetenland pleased those who believed Hitler's promises that he wouldn't make any further territorial claims, since it seemed that a new European war had been avoided. Hitler, however, had other ideas. When the German troops arrived in the Sudetenland, they were greeted by cheering crowds, but not everyone was happy to see them on Czech soil. Emil Hacha was installed as the new Czechoslovak president after the previous one, Benes, resigned, but in March 1939, not long after he took power, Hitler told him at a meeting that German troops would march into Czechoslovakia at 6am the following morning, March 15. He was given a stark choice—either tell the Czech Army not to resist, or the country would be destroyed. Under much duress, Hacha gave in and the next day silent crowds watched the German invaders march in.

Date:.......................March 7, 1936—German troops occupy the Rhineland
March 12/13, 1938—Germany announces Anschluss
(union) with Austria
October 15, 1938—German troops occupy Sudetenland &
the Czech government resigns
March 15/16, 1939—Nazis take Czechoslovakia
Participants: ....Rhineland:
Three battalions of unarmed troops
Anschluss:
General Guderian's XVI Army Corps
Sudetenland:
President Eduard Benes; German troops including the 1st,
2nd and 3rd Panzer Divisions
Czechoslovakia:
Generalfeldmarshall Fedor von Bock led German troops,
including the 3rd Panzer Division
Location of event:......Europe, from the Rhineland through Austria to
Czechoslovakia
Outcome:..................The world finally woke up to Hitler's intentions

Hitler and Mussolini in Venice, 1934.

MAY 22, 1939–AUGUST 23, 1939

Nazis sign "Pact of Steel" with Italy

On May 22, 1939, Hitler and Benito Mussolini signed the "Pact of Steel" in Berlin. This was a declaration of friendship and alliance—it committed Germany and Italy to a military alliance that formed what was known as the Axis powers. From Italy's perspective, hostilities were not expected for at least three years—as a result of participation in the Spanish Civil War her armies needed to be completely re-equipped. When Germany went to war much sooner than expected, Italy was unprepared, and did not fulfil her commitments under the treaty.

Soviet Foreign Commissar Vyacheslav Molotov signs the German-Soviet nonaggression pact; Joachim von Ribbentrop and Josef Stalin stand behind him. Moscow, August 23.

August 23, 1939—Nazis and Soviets sign pact

Hitler knew that he could not simultaneously fight a war with the Soviets as well as the Allies, even though he had every intention of invading Russia. He blamed the Soviets for colluding with the Jews to bring down Germany, and so wanted to end the Bolshevik regime. To buy some time, he arranged a non-aggression pact between Germany and Russia—this basically stated that after Poland had been invaded, Stalin and Hitler would divide the country up between them. Russia would also gain the Baltic states of Latvia and Estonia. The deal, which was known as either the Nazi-Soviet Pact or the Molotov-Ribbentrop Pact, was signed on August 23, 1939.

Date:	May 22, 1939—Nazis sign "Pact of Steel" with Italy
	August 23, 1939—Nazis and Soviets sign Pact
Participants:	Pact of Steel:
	The Italian Foreign Minister, Galeazzo Ciano
	The German foreign minister, Joachim von Ribbentrop
	Molotov-Ribbentrop Pact:
	The German foreign minister, Joachim von Ribbentrop
	The Soviet foreign minister, Vyacheslav Molotov
Location of event:	Pact of Steel:Berlin
	Molotov-Ribbentrop Pact:Moscow
Outcome:	Germany and the Soviet Union invaded Poland; the beginning of World War II

Germans invade Poland.

SEPTEMBER 1, 1939

When Hitler was ready to invade Poland, he once again used his security services to create a suitable excuse to send in troops. The ingenious Heydrich, head of intelligence and security in the SS, had some of his SS officers disguise themselves as Polish soldiers—they then attacked a German radio station in Gleiwicz. These soldiers announced on live radio that Poland was invading Germany, and Hitler suddenly had his pretext for invasion. German troops invaded Poland on September 1, 1939 and after Hitler rejected demands to withdraw, Britain and France declared war on Germany on September 3, 1939— World War II had begun. America decided that it could not afford to get involved—it had neither the political will, nor the desire to do so, and so it quickly proclaimed neutrality. Canada, Australia and New Zealand, however, stood by their European allies, and also declared war on Germany.

The invasion signalled the start of the largest military conflict in history. Germany poured military units into a beleaguered Poland, sending in troops from East Prussia and Germany in the north and Silesia and Slovakia in the south. They were backed by more than 2,000 tanks and over 1,000 aircraft. If Germany's continued invasion from the west wasn't bad enough for the Polish people, three weeks later the Soviet Union joined the conflict and sent armies into the country from the east. Poland could not withstand such an onslaught, and by the end of the month only Warsaw still held out. Much of the country lay in ruins, and on October 6, after a fierce onslaught, the city finally surrendered to the Germans. Poland was then split between Germany and Russia, who occupied territories either side of the line of the Bug River.

German troops parade through Warsaw, Poland.

German soldiers remove Polish street signs as part of the strategy of eridacating Polish culture.

Date: ....September 1, 1939, Nazis invade Poland; Russia attacks September 17, Britain, France, Australia, and New Zealand declare war on Germany. United States proclaims neutrality. Canada declares war on Germany

Participants: ....Polish armed forces, German Army Group North (Germany and East Prussia) and South (Silesia and Slovakia); latterly Russian Twentieth Army

Location of event: ......Initially north and west Poland; from 17th east and south

Outcome: ....Germany takes 73,000 sq. miles as a Reich Protectorate; Russia annexes 77,000 sq. miles

The defeated Finnish defenders of Kuhmo return home after the signing of the Finnish-Soviet peace accord.

April 9, 1940

With the fall of Poland, Hitler looked to the next stages of his territorial expansion. He postponed an attack westward, since copies of his invasion plans had fallen into Allied hands, but in the meantime he drove north. Scandinavia was of great strategic value—not only did Sweden provide much of Germany's iron ore but Norway's geographical positioning was of vital significance for naval control of the North Sea. Hitler knew that he had only so much time before it would become much more difficult to invade Scandinavia, for Britain was rapidly building up its military strength.

To complicate matters, Stalin's troops invaded Finland on November 30, 1939, and the Allies intended to send a force to help the Finns defend themselves. This would have put Allied troops in a position where they could threaten Germany's iron ore supply, but before this could happen a peace settlement was signed between Russia and Finland. In order to make sure that he had control of Norwegian naval bases, Hitler decided to invade Norway. He assembled a force of 100,000 troops, 71 ships, and 28 submarines for the surprise attack which he named the "Weser Exercise" or Weserübung. Although taking Norway was his main objective, Hitler decided to invade Denmark at the same time. His forces began the invasion on April 9, 1940, and he described the action as "the boldest and most impudent in the history of warfare." Sweden he did not invade: it was neutral but, initially, sympathetic to Nazism—surprisingly large numbers of Swedes entered the German armed forces and it was a good source of materials to Nazi Germany and, therefore, not part of Hitler's invasion plan of Scandinavia.

Denmark was over-run within two hours, for her forces were too small to stave off the heavy units of the German Army and air force; the

The Finnish population rapidly mobilized to dig infantry trench systems using the zig-zag configuration.

Dancs had no choice but to agree to an unconditional surrender. The Germans issued an ultimatum to the Norwegians, but the king refused to surrender. After several weeks of fierce fighting the lightly armed Norwegian Army (backed by small numbers of Allied troops) was beaten, and in mid-June 1940, Norway capitulated.

Date:..........................April 9, 1940
Participants: ....Norway:
　　　　　　　　3rd Mountain Division, 69th, 163rd, 196th, and 181st
　　　　　　　　Infantry Divisions, and the 11th Motorized Rifle Brigade
　　　　　　　　Denmark:
　　　　　　　　XXXI Corps under General der Flieger Leonard Kaupisch
　　　　　　　　170th, 198th, and 214th Infantry Divisions
　　　　　　　　170th Infantry Division and the 11th Motorized Rile
　　　　　　　　Brigade
　　　　　　　　Five warship groups, consisting of light naval craft, merchant
　　　　　　　　vessels, and the battleship Schleswig-Holstein
Location of event:......Norway and Denmark
Outcome: ....The occupation of Norway and Denmark

French prisoners of war prepare for a potato dinner, most were sent to Germany itself, voluntarily Frenchmen worked for Germany to escape living in occupied France.

MAY 10, 1940

Having successfully invaded Poland and Scandinavia, Hitler started on the western front, with the initial targets being Luxembourg, Belgium, Holland and France. In order to out-maneuver any possible mutual support agreements, he invaded Holland and Belgium first, since both countries were neutral.

On May 12, 1940, two days after the German armies invaded the Netherlands, Belgium and Luxembourg, they attacked France. Instead of coming through Belgium and northern France as they had done in World War I, however, their main thrust was through the Ardennes. This was a hilly and forested area that was considered by most to be completely unsuitable for armored military units. The plan, which was devised by General Erich von Manstein, took everyone by surprise. While they did send 29 divisions into Belgium, this was a diversionary attack and it drew all the Allied forces toward it. The main force, however, which was comprised of 40 divisions, came through further south; the French were totally unprepared for this maneuver, and their forces in the region collapsed.

Meanwhile, the combined efforts of the British Expeditionary Force and the main units of the French Army were totally overwhelmed as they tried to defend Belgium. The German tanks fought in close columns supported from the air by Stuka dive-bombers—an extremely effective form of warfare which became known as "lightning war," or Blitzkrieg. The Allied armies had never faced such tactics before, and they were not equipped to deal with such an onslaught. Indeed, their troops—and much of their military hardware—was totally outclassed by the well-trained soldiers and modern weapons of the Wehrmacht.

Adolf Hitler in Paris, June 23 1940.

On the same day that Germany attacked France, Neville Chamberlain was replaced by Winston Churchill as the British Prime Minister. This marked a sea change in the Allies' political attitude. Churchill was a fighter who had spoken out against appeasement in the interwar period: from this point forward there would be a tough military stance.

Date: .... May 10, 1940—Nazis invade France, Belgium, Luxembourg, and the Netherlands; Winston Churchill becomes British Prime Minister
May 15, 1940—Holland surrenders to the Nazis.
Participants: .... von Rundstedt's Army and the 7th Panzer Division under General Rommel
Location of event: ...... Western Europe
Outcome: .... The occupation of France, Belgium, Luxembourg, and the Netherlands
Winston Churchill becomes British Prime Minister

British prisoners at Dunkirk, France.

MAY 26, 1940

As the German armies moved through Belgium, the Belgian Army, nine divisions of the British Expeditionary Force, and ten divisions of the French First Army became pinned against the coast at Dunkirk, on the shores of the English Channel. Allied commanders had quickly realized that they could not hold such a strong enemy at bay, and so they prepared for the biggest evacuation ever attempted. For some reason, Hitler called his troops to halt their advances. Instead of moving in and finishing off the Allies, he called his tanks off. There are many theories as to why he did this. It is said that he wanted the Luftwaffe to finish the job, as the marshy ground near the coast was unsuitable for tank warfare. Another theory is that he wanted to give the British a chance to withdraw gracefully so that he could broker a peace deal with them. A third possibility is that his armies had moved so quickly that his supply lines had become too extended: the support columns could not keep up, and the armored units simply ran out of fuel. The most likely explanation is that all these issues had a bearing on Hitler's decision. Whatever the factors were, it gave the British the chance to mount the most incredible rescue mission in history.

Destroyed Allied vehicles on the beaches of Dunkirk.

The evacuation of Dunkirk was accomplished through a combination of factors. First, the Royal Air Force staged a frantic series of attacks against the Luftwaffe. This, together with bad weather, significantly reduced the effectiveness of the German air onslaught. When Hitler realized that the Luftwaffe was not able to do the job on its own, he ordered the tanks to move forward once again. Meanwhile, as 40,000 French troops did their best to hold out against the Germans, an evacuation fleet of 850 vessels—boats and ships of all sizes—crossed the Channel and rescued a total of 338,226 Allied troops.

Date: .... May 26, 1940—Evacuation of Allied troops from Dunkirk begins
Participants: .... British Expeditionary Force under General John Gort German forces under General Gerd von Rundstedt and General Heinz Guderian
Location of event: ...... Dunkirk, Belgium, and the English Channel
Outcome: .... The successful evacuation of 338,226 Allied troops

May 28, 1940—Belgium surrenders to the Nazis

In order to defend itself against German aggression, France had spent many years building a massive series of fortifications which became known as the Maginot Line. When the German armies invaded, however, most of the troops and armor went south of the line, through the Ardennes forest. Those that attacked Belgium on May 10 simply skirted around the north of the line where there were no defenses. The might of the onslaught caused huge numbers of refugees to flee, and this blocked the roads so effectively that the Allies were unable to move their armies forward. Belgium could not defend itself against the combination of tanks, air power, artillery and motorized infantry, and surrendered on May 28.

June 14, 1940—Germans enter Paris

Hitler knew that if he could take Paris, France would soon fall. The city was evacuated by the French government on June 13, and the next day the German armies moved in.

June 16, 1940—Marshal Pétain becomes French Prime Minister

Hitler was ecstatic that his advances westward had been a complete success, and he installed Marshal Phillippe Pétain in the south of France as a puppet governor, whose capital was the small town of Vichy. Hitler placed the rest of the country—approximately two-thirds of France—under German military administration.

German troops parade through Paris, France became the most popular foreign destination for German garisoned troops.

June 22, 1940—France signs an armistice with the Nazis

After World War I, Germany had been forced to take part in a humiliating surrender ceremony in a railway carriage at Compiègne. This had wounded the pride of the nation, and so when the French asked for an armistice on June 17, Hitler staged a massive propaganda event aimed at assuaging his country's anger. On June 22, he forced the French to sign an armistice in the full glare of the media—this was then replayed across the world to show that Germany had arisen from the ashes. It took place in the same carriage—hurriedly taken from the museum in which it had been preserved—at the same location.

Dates:	May 28, 1940—Belgium surrenders to the Nazis
	June 14, 1940—Germans enter Paris
	June 16, 1940—Marshal Pétain becomes French Prime Minister
	June 22, 1940—France signs an armistice with the Nazis
Participants:	Field Marshal von Rundstedt, commanding Army Group A
Location of event:	Belgium and France
Outcome:	The occupation of Belgium and northern France. The creation of the Vichy government in southern France under Marshal Phillippe Petain.

These Bristol Beaufighters were used in dedicated search of German night bombers.

JULY 10–SEPTEMBER 3, 1940

With much of mainland Europe under Nazi control, Hitler started the next phase—the invasion of Britain. On paper this should not have presented a significant problem—only the relatively narrow English Channel separated his forces from the shores of southern England. Britain also stood alone, her European allies all having fallen to the might of the German armies. Having only just come out of a major economic crisis, America wanted to stay out of the war.

Herman Göring assured Hitler that his Luftwaffe would soften up the British sufficiently for the invasion to be a forgone conclusion. In July 1940, Hitler ordered an invasion—it was to be launched in September, and code-named Operation "Sea Lion." Although Hitler was confident, his generals were less so. Moving large numbers of troops across the Channel would be tough enough, but if they attempted to do so against the full might of the British navy, it would be unthinkable. Hitler ordered that the Battle of Britain would take place—this would entail the Luftwaffe destroying as many of the British air and naval bases as possible, along with aircraft, ships, storage depots and any other relevant targets.

Although the Royal Air Force was outnumbered, with the secret development of radar and the accuracy of the Ultra information, it had a technical advantage. Having early warning of the approach of German aircraft meant that the British could use their smaller numbers of fighter aircraft extremely effectively. They took an enormous toll of German fighters and bombers—whose numbers belied their shortcomings. By the end of August, Luftwaffe Chief Hermann Göring realized that he needed to focus his forces on the destruction of the RAF before they could go back to their other targets. The RAF could not hold out against the

London ruins from bombing - "One of Goering's 'Military' Objectives".

entire might of the Luftwaffe, and was in real trouble. It was only when German aircraft accidentally bombed some civilian homes in London that things changed. In retaliation, British aircraft bombed Berlin the next night, and this so angered Hitler that the Luftwaffe was ordered to switch its attentions from attacking the RAF to the wholesale bombing of British cities. This unexpected respite allowed the RAF to rebuild itself, and having failed to take control of British airspace, on September 17 Hitler postponed Operation "Sea Lion."

Dates:	July 10, 1940—The Battle of Britain begins
	September 3, 1940—Hitler plans Operation "Sea Lion," the invasion of Britain
Participants:	Royal Air Force and Luftwaffe
Location of event:	The skies of southeast England
Outcome:	The cancellation of the invasion of Britain, Operation "Sea Lion"

Adolf Hitler addressing the Nazi party.

SEPTEMBER 27, 1940

The Tripartite Pact was signed in Berlin on September 27, 1940 by Germany, Italy, and Japan. It was basically a formal agreement that tied the Axis partners together—its initial intent was to keep America out of the war for as long as possible, although it was later extended to also cover other agendas.

The inclusion of Yugoslavia in the Tripartite Pact came about as a result of Mussolini's jealousy of Germany's territorial expansion. He decided to show Hitler that Italy could do just as well on its own, and on October 28, 1940, Italian troops set about invading Greece. Mussolini, however, had underestimated his opponents, and with Allied help the Greeks pushed his troops back. Hitler was furious about not being told in advance about the attack, but had little option but to reinforce the Italian operation—the last thing he needed was an Allied presence near the Romanian oilfields.

To mount an invasion of Greece, German forces would have to cross the Balkans—the best route from a military point of view was through

Mussolini parades with his generals.

Emperor Hirohito Dressed in Military Attire.

Yugoslavia. This would be very difficult to arrange, however, as not only was there strong anti-Nazi feeling in the country, but the British were desperately trying to persuade the Yugoslavs to resist German pressure. After much political effort, Hitler managed to create the Tripartite Pact, in which Yugoslavia would be given the Greek port of Salonika, no territory would be ceded to Germany, and no German troops would travel through the country.

This was finally signed by Prince Paul of Yugoslavia on March 24, 1941 (Slovakia had signed in November 1940; Croatia in June 1941). However, the Serbians staged a massive revolt and the Prince was forced to resign. The Balkan part of the hard-won pact collapsed, and Hitler raged that the country must be destroyed. The Tripartite Pact was later joined by Hungary on November 20, 1940, Romania on November 23, 1940, and Bulgaria on March 1, 1941.

Date: .... September 27, 1940
Participants: .... Representatives of Nazi Germany, Italy, and Japan
Location of event: ...... Berlin
Outcome: .... Improved relations between Germany and Japan; a warning to the United States to stay out of the war

Italian battleship Caio Duillio lies crippled in Taranto harbor.

November 11-12, 1940

In 1940 the Allies had a serious problem—although they had massive naval power, the British Mediterranean Fleet commanded by Admiral Andrew Cunningham was outnumbered by the Italian navy. The Italians had six battleships and more vessels in every class than the British, except aircraft carriers.

Winston Churchill was well aware that if German ships reinforced those of the Italians it would make the situation much worse, and so he ordered an air attack on the Italian fleet at its base in Taranto, on the south coast of Italy. The RAF mounted reconnaissance flights using aircraft from Allied bases in Malta, and their pilots confirmed that the whole Italian fleet was moored up. Code-named Operation "Judgement," the attack was scheduled for the night of November 11-12, 1940.

The original plans stipulated that 36 Swordfish torpedo bombers would attack; however, on the day only 24 were available. Two waves went in, each composed of 12 aircraft. Three aircraft were lost en route from the second wave, and so only 21 aircraft actually reached the target. Although the Swordfish was a dated design of aircraft, it was ideal for low-speed torpedo attacks on shipping. The Fleet Air Arm crews chosen for the attack were highly experienced, and five torpedoes hit three battleships—these were the Vittorio Veneto, the Caio Duilio and the Conte di Cavour. The daring operation was an outstanding success, and overnight it halved the functional strength of the Italian navy. Only two British aircraft were lost, and in the words of Admiral Andrew Cunningham:

"Taranto, and the night of November 11-12, 1940, should be remembered for ever as having shown once and for all that in the Fleet Air Arm the Navy has its most devastating weapon."

Oil gushes from Italian warships following the torpedo strikes by the British Swordfish bombers.

Date:.........................November 11 and 12, 1940
Participants: ....24 Fairey Swordfish torpedo bombers, nicknamed
                            "Stringbags" launched from the Royal Navy's carrier HMS
                            Illustrious
Location of event:......Taranto, Italy
Outcome: ....The crippling of the Italian fleet; Japan had a template for
                            the attack on Pearl Harbor

Italian column moves along a North African coastal road.

DECEMBER 9–10, 1940

When Germany started its offensive in Europe, Mussolini watched Germany's territorial expansion with envy. He realized, however, that although the two countries were allies, Hitler would not share out his gains unless Italy had something to offer in return. Mussolini, therefore, wanted to make some territorial gains too. Since his attack on Greece had gone badly, and most of the rest of Europe had already been taken by Germany, Mussolini decided to try to expand southward into Africa. When Italy declared war against Britain and France on June 10, 1940, there were 200,000 Italian troops in Libya and 250,000 in Ethiopia and Italian-held Somalia. Against these massive numbers, the British had only 40,000 men under the command of General Archibald Wavell in North Africa.

The Italians, who were commanded by Marshal d'Armata Rodolfo Graziani, invaded and occupied British Somalia on August 17, 1940—this was a serious blow as it threatened to cut off Allied access to India through the Suez Canal. Mussolini then ordered attacks to be made against British-occupied Egypt, and on September 13 Graziani reluctantly invaded Egypt. He made little progress, and on December 9 Wavell sent General Richard O'Connor and 30,000 men to retake Sidi Barrani, a small town in Egypt 65 miles from the border with Libya. Although they had fortified the town, most of the Italian forces were simple peasant conscripts who just wanted to go home to their farms. To make matters worse, their hardware was not designed to deal with desert conditions, and their defense soon fell apart. The British took 20,000 prisoners at Sidi Barrani, but General O'Connor decided to continue his attack and turned his raid into a full-scale invasion of Libya. He succeeded in occupying Tobruk and Benghazi, and took the whole of Cyrenaica as well as 130,000 Italian prisoners.

Italian troops of one of 43 divisions of infantry in North Africa.

A British battery of 25-Pounder field guns attacks enemy positions in Egypt.

Date:..........................December 9–10, 1940
Participants: ....Italian Fifth and Tenth Armies under Marshal Rodolfo
                          Graziani
                          British Western Desert Force under General Sir Archibald
                          Wavell
Location of event:......Egypt, Libya, Ethiopia, and Somalia
Outcome: ....The Italians failed to secure the port of Alexandria and the
                          Suez Canal, and their defeat caused Hitler to send in the
                          Afrika Korps to try and remedy the situation

Generalfeldmarschall Erwin Rommel, 'The Desert Fox' surveys the battlefield from his Mercedes Benz.

FEBRUARY 12–14, 1941

At the end of 1940, the British struck back against the Italians in North Africa and drove them out of Egypt and back into Libya. Once again, Hitler realized that he would have to pull the Italians out of another potential military disaster, and dispatched General Rommel with his Afrika Korps to sort the matter out.

As far as Hitler was concerned, there were two main priorities—first, he had his eyes on the oilfields of the Middle East. The German armies were heavily mechanized, and therefore were dependant on good access to fuel. Second, he wanted to ensure that the British did not take control of North Africa, as this would have left the entire southern coast of Europe open to attack. He could not afford to defend such a long front without sacrificing large numbers of his troops who were badly needed to invade Russia.

The British now faced a long and arduous task—what equipment they had left was largely worn out, and their supply chains were impossibly long. It would prove to be a long time before enough supplies arrived to help them cope with fighting Rommel's elite Afrika Korps troops. The wily German commander quickly developed new methods of fighting in the desert environment. One of the most effective techniques he adopted was the use of 88mm anti-aircraft guns on the open battlefields. These were used to devastating effect against tanks and armored vehicles, and formed a central part of the Blitzkrieg tactics he employed to outflank the British on many occasions.

The Germans did not have it all their own way, however. The British had a much better understanding of the terrain, and their intelligence network was far superior to that of their opponents. On top of this,

Generalfeldmarschall Erwin Rommel, Blue Max and Knights Cross holder, instrumental in the Fall of France 1940, commander of the Afrika Korps and German defences in western Europe.

British crypotanalysts had managed to crack the Nazi communications codes, and this gave them a tremendous advantage on the battlefield. When the Americans finally entered the war their industrial might provided an enormous boost to the British campaign in North Africa, and enough supplies arrived to turn the tide against Rommel and his troops.

Date:.........................February 12, 1941—Rommel arrives
February 14, 1941—First units of German Afrika Korps arrive
Participants: ....General Erwin Rommel arrived with one Panzer Division and one Motorised Infantry Division. These were supported by the Italian Ariete and Trento Divisions which arrived from Italy along with the Brescia Infantry Division
Location of event:......Tripoli, Libya
Outcome: ....The North African Desert Campaign continued until 1943

Aircraft ready for shipping from America as part of the lend lease act.

MARCH 11, 1941

After the fall of France in June 1940, Britain was left on its own to fight the spreading menace of Nazi aggression. At this stage Germany had been re-arming for years. Britain, however, was still trying to recover from the effects of the Great Depression. As a result the government had allowed much of the armed services to become depleted. The navy was particularly badly affected by the Treasury's decision not to build any new warships, and when the war began there were insufficient vessels to cope with the vast scale of the conflict. The sheer volume of production needed to catch up was beyond the resources of British industry, and appeals were made to the United States for help.

For a long time the Americans did not want to help, and it is certain that this had a major effect on the course of the early stages of the war. Gradually the U.S. attitude changed, although the initial terms the Americans outlined were felt to be unreasonable—in return for supplying military equipment, America wanted the entire British West Indies to be handed over. The naval bases there alone were worth more than Britain was asking for, and so the discussions stalled. It was President Franklin D. Roosevelt who finally managed to persuade Congress that fighting the Nazis by helping Britain was far better than fighting them on American soil.

Various motorized vehicles on their way to Britain courtesy of President Roosevelt.

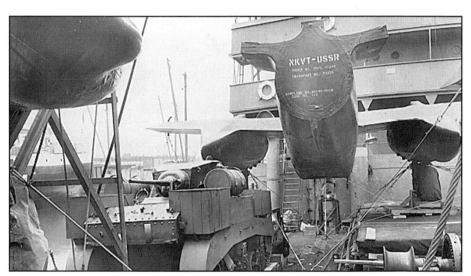

Tanks and Armored vehicles being shipped to Britain as part of the $50 billion dollars worth of military equipmnt supplied under the lend lease act.

As a result of Roosevelt's support, Congress passed the Lend-Lease Act on March 11, 1941. This provided Britain and 37 other countries with $50 billion worth of military equipment; however, it all had to be paid for when the war was over. Many in Congress refused to believe that Britain had been bankrupted by World War I, and as a result imposed exceedingly harsh financial terms on the $31 billion she received. These included the hand-over of British bases in Newfoundland, Bermuda and the West Indies. In the 21st century Britain is still repaying the loan.

Date:.........................March 11, 1941
Participants: ....President Franklin D. Roosevelt and the U.S. Congress made equipment and materials available to 38 different countries
Location of event:......U.S. Congress, Washington
Outcome: ....The British and their allies were able to obtain enough military hardware to fight the Axis powers

A Junkers JU-52 is shot down over the Northern coastline of Crete.

April 6–27, 1941

The failed Italian attempt to invade Greece had left Hitler with little option but to step in and recover the situation. If Greece fell to the Allies, it would put their troops too close to the vital Romanian oilfields for comfort. His dilemma, however, was just how he was going to get his troops to Greece across several countries that were outside his control. On March 24, 1941, he'd finally managed to get Prince Paul of Yugoslavia to sign the Tripartite Pact ; however, the Serbians—influenced by British Intelligence—staged a massive revolt and the Prince was forced to resign.

Hitler was furious and raged that Yugoslavia "must be regarded as an enemy and beaten down as soon as possible." He postponed Operation "Barbarossa"—the invasion of Russia—and went to war with both Greece and Yugoslavia. He gave precise instructions for the attack—two strategic groups would swoop on Belgrade and destroy the Yugoslav Army and Serbian Macedonia would be attacked by a third group.

Hitler then detailed how the destruction of Belgrade would be carried out, and on April 6, 1941, the Luftwaffe followed his orders by bombing the city for three days and three nights, reducing it to ruins. Shortly afterward German troops simultaneously invaded both Greece and Yugoslavia, backed by extra troops provided by Mussolini in the form of his Second and Eleventh Armies, who attacked from Albania. Hungary also joined in, having been promised that its claims for territories in Yugoslavia would be fulfilled. The combined might of all these forces quickly overwhelmed the Yugoslav Army, which was poorly led, low on morale and equipped with obsolete weaponry.

A Fallschirmjäger dressed in combat gear during operation "Mercury", the airborne invasion of Crete.

Yugoslavia capitulated on April 17 and around 340,000 officers and men became prisoners of war. The Germans lost 151 soldiers killed and had 15 listed as missing. The full effect of the Axis forces was then focused on Greece, and the mainland capitulated on April 23.

Dates:	April 6, 1941—Nazis invade Greece and Yugoslavia
	April 17, 1941—Yugoslavia surrenders to the Nazis
	April 27, 1941—Greece surrenders to the Nazis.
Participants:	German Second and Twelfth Armies.
	The Allies:
	6th Australian Division under Major General Ivan Mackay
	2nd New Zealand Division under Major General Sir Bernard Freyberg, VC
	British 1st Armoured Brigade
	Greek Army consisting of 21 divisions
	Poorly equipped Yugoslav Army
Location of event:	Greece and Yugoslavia
Outcome:	Greece and Yugoslavia fell to the Axis; the German invasion of Russia was delayed, with serious consequences

Hess and Hitler in Munich before World War II.

MAY 10, 1941

Rudolf Hess was one of Hitler's most trusted confidantes, and when the Nazis came to power in 1933 he was elevated to the rank of cabinet minister and became Hitler's dedicated deputy. Over the next few years he rarely left Hitler's side; however, as time went on, he found that his personal secretary, Martin Bormann, was starting to gain Hitler's attention, thus edging Hess out of favor.

In an attempt to regain his Führer's approval, Hess tried to broker a peace deal with the British, and made a surprise solo flight to Scotland in a Messerschmitt Bf110. He arrived there unexpectedly in May 1941, where he was immediately arrested. He told his captors that he was seeking peace between Germany and Britain so that they could join forces to fight the Communist threat from the Soviet Union; Churchill, however, refused to see Hess.

Back in Germany, Hitler was so angered by Hess's activities that he declared him mentally unconscious and abolished the post of Deputy Führer. He then made Martin Bormann the Head of the Party Chancellery in his place.

There is some doubt, however, as to whether Hitler was indeed ignorant of Hess's mission. Some claim that it was actually the Führer's idea in the first place—a few days before the flight the two had had a secret and heated meeting that lasted four hours. When the attempt at brokering a peace deal failed, though, Hitler wanted to wash his hands of the whole affair, and publicly rebuked Hess. In private, however, Hitler went to great efforts to protect Hess's family. It may never be known what the truth of the matter is—Hess was imprisoned by the Allies at Spandau Prison, West Berlin, until his death in 1987.

After his flight to Britain, Hess was kept in prison—at first in Britain and postwar in Spandau—until he killed himself in 1987.

Date:..........................May 10, 1941
Participants: ....Rudolf Hess, at the time nominally successor designate to Hitler after Göring
Location of event:......Flew Bf110 from Messerschmitt company HQ at Augsburg to Eaglesham, Scotland
Outcome: ....Hess imprisoned in Tower of London and sentenced to life imprisonment at Nuremberg Trials

HMS Hood entering Scapa flow.

MAY 24TH, 1941

When World War II began, Britain's particular geographical location presented it with both strengths and weaknesses. On the one hand, as an island, any foreign powers wanting to invade would first have to move their armies across the English Channel. In order to defend themselves, the British had kept a powerful navy for centuries. On the other hand, until the advent of the aeroplane, all Britain's imports also had to be transported by ship. This left it extremely vulnerable to naval blockades, something that Hitler wanted to exploit to the full by using his Kriegsmarine to starve the British into submission.

A major instrument in this operation was the Bismarck—the flagship of Hitler's fleet which had been launched on February 14, 1939. Although it was officially listed as being only 35,000 tons, to comply with the London Naval Treaty, it was in fact, at 50,900 tons, a similar size to HMS Hood—Britain's largest warship. The two battleships were, however, from different eras—HMS Hood was a vestige of the immediate post World War I period, whereas the Bismarck was brand new and built to the very latest designs. The Hood had very out-dated gunnery systems when compared with the Bismarck, which with far better armor could also absorb a lot more damage.

After being commissioned, the German naval command wanted to get the Bismarck into the Atlantic so that her awesome firepower could be used against Allied merchant shipping. In order to do this, however, she had to navigate her way past the British Isles—something that Churchill was determined to try to prevent. A massive amount of effort was put into monitoring her movements, and when she sailed past Norway into the Denmark Strait, HMS Hood intercepted her. At 05.52am on May 24, 1941, the Hood opened fire.

HMS Hood engages the Bismarck.

Two minutes later the Bismarck fired back, and within a very short time the Hood's magazine blew up and she sank with the loss of more than 1,400 lives.

The Bismarck did not escape unhurt, however, and over the following 72 hours the Royal Navy hunted her down, and with assistance from Swordfish torpedo bombers slowly blew her apart. It is thought that 2,131 men died from her complement and only 115 survived.

Date: .... May 24, 1941
Participants: .... German forces under Grand Admiral Erich Raeder and
Admiral Günther Lütjens:
Bismarck, under Kapitän zur See Ernst Lindemann
Prinz Eugen, under Kapitän zur See Helmuth Brinkmann
British forces under Admiral Tovey, Commander-in-
Chief of the British Home Fleet:HMSs Suffolk, Norfolk,
Birmingham, Manchester, Electra, Anthony, Echo, Icarus,
Achates, Antelope, Rodney, Sheffield, King George V. HMS
Hood under Captain Ralph Kerr. HMS Prince of Wales
under Captain John C Leach. HMS Dorsetshire. Swordfish
aircraft from HMSs Victorious and Ark Royal
Location of event: ...... Initially the Denmark Strait
Outcome: .... Hitler lost all trust in his surface fleet and as a result it never
became a threat to Allied Atlantic shipping

German soldiers engage in city fighting during operatioon "Barbarossa".

JUNE 22, 1941

After Hitler had finished with matters in the Balkans in the spring of 1941, he turned his attention toward Russia. Although the invasion of Greece and Yugoslavia had been successful, it had cost him valuable time. Since his dealings with the Russians were getting steadily worse, he could not afford to wait for spring the next year to launch Operation "Barbarossa," and so on June 22, 1941 he sent his armies east and onto Russian soil. The ensuing battle was the largest in modern history, with over 3 million men, more than 7,000 artillery pieces, 3,300 tanks, 600,000 vehicles, 2,770 aircraft, and 625 horses taking part. Hitler thought that with an army of this size, he could win the war in just 10 weeks.

Incredibly, Stalin was taken completely by surprise—both Roosevelt and Churchill had tried to warn him of the impending invasion, but his suspicious nature led him to believe it was an Allied ruse to break up the Russo-German Pact. At first the Germans made massive territorial gains—on the first day, three Russian infantry divisions were wiped out and another five were all but destroyed. The Luftwaffe destroyed 2,000 Russian aircraft, many of which were still on the ground.

What Hitler had not realized, however, was that Stalin had Russia's ultimate defense on his side—sheer land mass. He could afford to give away massive areas at little cost to himself. The German armies, however, could not possibly hope to take full control of these areas and supply their forces at the same time. There were very few paved roads in Russia, and so the heavily mechanized German Army was at the mercy of the weather; one spell of rain would turn the entire region into a mud-bath. The vast forests and marshes also disoriented the Germans, who found it hard to cope with the enormous scale of the land they were trying to conquer; they were in for a long and drawn-out fight.

A German officer blows the whistle for an attack. Note the fur hat, which was essential equipment for the harsh soviet winters.

Date: .... June 22, 1941
Participants: .... German Army Group North headed for Leningrad
Army Group Center headed for Moscow
Army Group South headed into the Ukraine
Red Army with Josef Stalin, as Supreme Commander-in-Chief and Georgi Zhukov as Chief of Staff.
Location of event: ...... The western regions of the Soviet Union from the borders to Leningrad, Moscow and southeast towards the Ukraine
Outcome: .... Leningrad surrounded and Kiev taken, along with much of the Ukraine

A platoon of German troops moves through a town on their way towards Moscow.

OCTOBER 2–DECEMBER 5, 1941

In September 1941, Hitler and his generals argued over how the armies should proceed. His High Command wanted to take Moscow—by securing the city, the German armies would have a safe haven in which they would be able to sit out the harsh winter. Since it was the capital city, it also had major importance as a communications and armaments production center. On top of this, most of the Russian transport systems ran through Moscow—control of the city would be a major disruption to Russian logistics. Hitler, however, thought that capturing the oil and coal fields in southern Russia was more important. In the end Hitler agreed with his staff officers, and decided that their forces should engage in a major push for Moscow. The offensive was code-named Operation "Typhoon."

By early October, Hitler had amassed troops from across the entire eastern front, and as soon as they were ready he sent them in against the Soviet defenses. The Russians were taken completely by surprise as it did not make military sense to mount an offensive so late in the year. Their lines quickly crumbled, and 600,000 men were taken prisoner. German armored columns then raced toward Moscow, but quickly ran into fierce resistance. To make matters worse, the weather also turned against them, and the rains came. The entire area became a quagmire, and the mechanized advance ground to a halt only 40 miles from Moscow. When the rains stopped, the troops moved forward again; however, by the time they reached the gates of Moscow, they had insufficient strength to break through. The Red Army mounted a counter-offensive, and this, together with the onset of the severe Russian winter, meant that the Germans had to abandon any idea of taking Moscow, and instead begin a long and protracted withdrawal from Moscow.

Russian troops fighting German troops in Moscow.

Dates: .... October 2, 1941—Operation "Typhoon" begins
December 5, 1941—The attack on Moscow is abandoned.
Participants: .... German forces under the Supreme Command of the Army
(OKH):
The Army Group Center, comprising 50 infantry divisions,
14 armored divisions, 8 mechanized divisions, 4 security
divisions and 5 brigades
Second, Fourth, and Ninth Armies
Second, Third, and Fourth Armored Groups
2nd Air Fleet
Group Moskau, designed to identify and exterminate the
state and party authorities of the Soviet Union and any
political or cultural activists
The Russian armed forces:
Army Group West, commanded by Marshal Semyon
Timoshenko and later by General Georgiy Zhukov
Army Group Bryansk, commanded by General Andrei
Yeremenko
Reserve Army Group, commanded by Marshal Semyon
Budyonny
24,000 Muscovite civilians
Location of event: ...... Moscow
Outcome: .... 600,000 Russian troops captured in initial advances. The
German armies then got bogged down by fierce resistance
and the harsh Russian winter on the outskirts of Moscow

Female combatants in Moscow used in skilled roles such as snipers, pilots and tank drivers.

December 6, 1941

In his haste to attack Stalin, Hitler had not considered what would happen if his troops did not manage to capture Moscow. On December 4, 1941, the day after his armies arrived at the gates of Moscow, to the utter astonishment of the German High Command, the Soviets launched a massive winter counter-offensive. Hitler believed that the Russians had run out of men and equipment, so when the Germans were suddenly faced with 100 fresh divisions of men, it was a massive shock.

The German troops had not been equipped to cope with the harsh Russian winter. Hitler had refused to issue winter clothing as he wanted to give his men an incentive to try their best to take Moscow. As a result of this they still had their thin summer uniforms and were completely unprepared for their predicament. As they began a protracted withdrawal over the next few months, many tens of thousands of German soldiers literally froze to death. By January 1942, they had been forced back a total of around 200 miles.

Stalin had many objectives during this period. Not only did he want to beat the enemy on the battlefield but he also wanted to demonstrate to his people and to the world that the Germans were far from invincible. Knowing that Hitler's armies were in a bad state, suffering from the effects of the harsh winter as well as from a lack of food and equipment, Stalin simply kept attacking them over and over again. He used fresh troops wherever possible on the basis that it would keep the maximum pressure on the German armies, a philosophy that worked extremely well. For the first time in the war, Hitler was not having it all his own way.

Heavily armed Soviet troops with PPSH41 sub-machine guns.

Russian army building defences behind retreating Germans

Date:..........................December 6, 1941
Participants: ....Marshal Georgi Konstantinovich Zhukov commanded 88
infantry divisions, and 15 cavalry divisions of fresh troops
brought from Siberia and the far East to Moscow. These
included Soviet Thirty-third andThirty-ninth Armies made
up of combined tank and cavalry groupings as well as large
Cossack units.
Location of event:......Mosow, Soviet Union
Outcome: ....The siege of Leningrad by German troops was broken

Battleship Row after the suprise Japanese attack on Pearl Harbor.

DECEMBER 7, 1941

In the years leading up to the beginning of the war Japan was becoming increasingly industrialized. However, this left it in a difficult situation as it did not have enough raw materials to keep the economy going. One of the commodities the country needed especially badly was oil, and when the Japanese seized southern Indochina in the early years of the war, America's reaction was to slap an oil embargo on the Japanese. Since oil was such a vital component in Japan's industrial and military machines, this was seen as an act of war. America was only too aware that war was inevitable—indeed, Roosevelt was desperate for an excuse to enter the war. He was unable to do so without provocation, however, as his election had depended on a commitment to stay out of conflict unless the U.S. was attacked.

The U.S. Pacific Fleet was moved to its naval base at Pearl Harbor in Hawaii. However, all the aircraft carriers and other modern ships were kept at sea well out of range of Japanese aircraft. This left Pearl Harbor, which was halfway between America and the nearest Japanese military bases, full of antiquated, obsolete ships.

The Japanese decided that a surprise attack would give them the military advantage they needed if they were going to take on a nation with a navy the size of that of the United States. As a result, Admiral Isoroku Yamamoto, Commander-in-Chief of Japan's Combined Fleet, drew up a plan to deliver a knockout attack on the United States Pacific Fleet. This would leave the Japanese free to launch their offensive against the British, American and Dutch forces in southeast Asia. If all went well, the attack could possibly even force America to accept a peace deal, leaving Japan in charge of the Pacific region.

Kaneohe Naval Air Station in flames following the Japanese aerial assault.

On the morning of December 7, 1941 Yamamoto launched his offensive on a completely unprepared Pearl Harbor. Japan had not made a formal declaration of war but it began when 353 aircraft took off from aircraft carriers belonging to the Japanese Imperial Navy. Although more than half the U.S. fleet was at sea, there were still around 100 ships of all sizes moored in the harbor. When the Japanese aircraft reached Oahu, they attacked nearby airfields as well as the harbor. This prevented all but a handful of American fighters taking off to defend the island—even so, 29 Japanese aircraft were shot down by the combined efforts of these brave pilots and antiaircraft gunners on the ground. When the attack was over, the toll included eight battleships damaged, of which five had been sunk. Eleven smaller vessels were also badly damaged—these included cruisers and destroyers. The human casualty count included 2,335 servicemen and 68 civilians killed, and 1,178 people injured. The attack was a serious shock to the American people, and this anger provided Roosevelt with the excuse he needed to bring the United States into the war. Whether he deliberately set up and sacrificed Pearl Harbor is still being debated by the historians.

Date:..........................December 7, 1941
Participants: ....The attack was planned by Admiral Isoroku Yamamoto
Eighteenth Army Air Corps aircraft were led by Commander Mitsuo Fuchida
Japanese Imperial Navy
U.S. Pacific Fleet
Location of event:......Pearl Harbor, Oahu, Hawaii
Outcome: ....The Americans lost eight battleships damaged, of which five were sunk. Eleven smaller vessels were also badly damaged— these included cruisers and destroyers. 2,335 servicemen and 68 civilians were killed, and 1,178 injured. U.S. declared war shortly after
The Japanese lost 29 aircraft to ground fire and U.S. pilots

Japanese planes fly over island under surrender - Hong Kong.

DECEMBER 7–31, 1941

When the Japanese started making their plans for war, they had two priorities. The first was to invade and secure countries with good sources of the raw materials needed to keep the military machine going. The second was to take the key strategic areas needed to ensure that the Allies would not be able to threaten these new Japanese interests. They were especially keen on capturing Java's oilfields. Otherwise, even if they reduced their usage to a minimum, the American oil embargo would leave them with enough supplies for only three years, after which the country would grind to a halt. Malaya's tin mines and vast rubber plantations were also needed, and many of the smaller islands in the Far East were rich in other mineral and agricultural resources.

The Japanese territorial expansion began at the same time as the attack on Pearl Harbor on December 7, 1941. It started with invasions of Siam, Malaya and Hong Kong. Malaya fell far more easily than it should have done—this was as a result of the complacency of the British Regular Army and its entrenched arrogance toward the Japanese military capability. The British soon found out to their cost how wrong they had been. On top of this, the three services—the Army, air force and navy—were intense rivals, and unable and unwilling to work together. As a result the Army could not defend the RAF's airfields, the RAF's aircraft were all obsolete, and the navy wrongly believed that its fleet was invincible.

Burma was invaded on December 11, 1941—this was for strategic purposes rather than for the country's resources. The invasion was intended to curtail the risk that the British would be able to strike back at the Japanese forces in Malaya, to put a stop to the transport of supplies by the U.S. to China along the Burma Road, and also to provide a

Japanese troops come ashore on Malaya.

stepping stone for an invasion of India. By May 1942 the Japanese had taken the entire country. At the end of December 1941, the Japanese had used their superior equipment and training to also invade Borneo, the Philippines and Wake Island.

Dates:	December 7,1941 Japan invades Siam, Malaya, Hong Kong
	December 11,1941 Japan invades Burma
	December 16,1941 Japan invades Borneo
	December 22,1941 Japan invades Philippines
	December 23,1941 Japan invades Wake Island
	December 24,1941 Battle of Makassar Strait
	December 25,1941 Hong Kong surrenders
	December 31,1941 Japan occupies Manila
Participants:	Japanese Imperial Army and Navy
Location of event:	Southeast Asia
Outcome:	Most of the Asia-Pacific region was overrun by Japanese forces

President Roosevelt signs the act declaring war on Japan.

German U-Boats depart on their mission to disrupt merchant shipping in the Atlantic.

DECEMBER 8, 1941

With the Japanese attack on Pearl Harbor December 7, 1941, President Roosevelt at last had the perfect excuse to bring the U.S. into the war. He had been trying to provoke either Germany or Japan into attacking American interests for some considerable time, as he was desperate to ensure that Nazi Germany did not manage to take the whole of Europe and Russia. It was quite clear to him that if it did, the U.S. would be its next target, and he would far rather fight the Nazis on foreign soil than his own. He was in a difficult position, however, as he had made strong pledges to the American people during his election campaign that he would keep their sons out of the war. Much to his frustration, both Germany and Japan did all they could to avoid any actions that could be construed as aggression against the US. In the end, the American oil embargo forced the Japanese to act, as their economy would completely collapse without new supplies. When the attack on Pearl Harbor came, Roosevelt and Churchill presented a united front and jointly declared war on Japan.

The very same day that America's declaration was made, Hitler declared war on the United States. One of the terms of the Tripartite Act was that if another nation attacked Japan, Germany would then also be at war with that country. Churchill knew then that the war was won—Germany could not possibly compete with the industrial might of America. Even though there would be many battles to fight, if a straightforward war of attrition was waged the outcome was inevitable—sooner or later, Germany would run out of men, supplies and equipment. The war then moved to the very shores of America when German U-boats began attacking merchant shipping along its east coast in January 1942.

Dates: ....December 8, 1941—United States and Britain declare war on Japan
December 11, 1941—Germany declares war on the United States
Participants: ....President Roosevelt, Winston Churchill, Adolf Hitler
Location of event:......In Germany:The Reichstag, Berlin, Germany
In Britain:The Houses of Parliament
In the U.S.:The Senate and House of Representatives, The White House
Outcome: ....The European war becomes a world war

DECEMBER 19TH, 1941

In December 1941, Adolf Hitler took over complete command of the complicated hierarchy of the German Army. The story behind this is long and complicated, but in essence, the army's senior staff officers had been a thorn in Hitler's side for many years. For a start, he had never risen above the rank of corporal, and so was looked down on as a social and military upstart by the aristocratic German officer elite. Whenever Hitler had put forward plans for military expansion, they tried to oppose him. This included the remilitarization of the Rhineland, the occupation of Austria and Czechoslovakia as well as the invasions of Poland, France and the Soviet Union. On top of this all the attempts to overthrow Hitler originated in the army. He had tolerated this since he first came to prominence because he relied on the army's backing to remain in power.

By 1941, however, Hitler was growing tired of continually having to argue with his high command over every small detail of military strategy. He was also painfully aware that during World War One a military dictatorship had developed, and therefore wanted to ensure that the same thing could not happen again. When the German Army failed to capture

Eastern Front German troops with howitzer.

Moscow and the Soviet counteroffensive began, his Commander in Chief, von Brauchitsch, suffered a heart attack and Hitler took advantage of the situation to personally take over.

By taking direct command of the army, he was able to divide up the individual theatres of operations within the military arena so that he was the only person who knew what was happening across the board. This weakened the army leadership's position significantly, although its opposition to Hitler continued until the end of the war.

Date:.........................December 19, 1941
Participants: ....Adolf Hitler, Field Marshal von Brauchitsch
Location of event:......Wolfschanze —The Wolf's Lair, Rastenburg, East Prussia
                        (now Poland)
Outcome: ....von Brauchitsch never returned to active service;
                        Hitler's insistence on no retreats would later destroy the
                        German Army in Russia

German aerial reconnaissance photograph of an Atlantic convoy of Allied support ships.

In the Tripartite Pact, Hitler had made an agreement to declare war on any country that attacked any of the other signatory members. As a result of the Japanese assault on Pearl Harbor on December 7, 1941, Germany was bound by the terms of the pact to declare war on the United States, something that Hitler had been trying to delay for as long as possible. On December 11, 1941, he did so, and this lifted the previous restrictions on German U-boats attacking American shipping. Operation "Drumbeat" (Paukenschlag) was then put into action—this was the launch of a U-boat offensive which specifically sought out and attacked American shipping along the east coast of the United States.

Although Admiral Dönitz originally planned for 12 U-boats to travel across the Atlantic Ocean to strike against their intended targets, Hitler wanted six of them to be used elsewhere. Of the remaining six, one was undergoing major repairs, and so he had only five of his long-range submarines available. Although it was planned that the U-boats would be in position to begin their operations on January 13, 1942, one of the five—U-123—arrived two days early. Her captain immediately set about his task, and sunk the first ship he encountered—this turned out to be the 9,000-ton British freighter SS Cyclops. When the other four U-boats joined in, they sank an average of one ship a day until the operation finished on February 6, 1942. This amounted to a total of 25 vessels, which when combined came to a massive 156,939 tons. This was a massive blow to the Allied war effort and to the morale of both the American and British people.

After Operation "Drumbeat" was completed, many other U-boats crossed the Atlantic to take part in the slaughter. They sank a huge number of ships throughout the Gulf of Mexico and the Caribbean, with

An arctic convoy escort ship, its guns inopperable until the ice had been chipped off.

German Navy - submarine deck, gun covered in ice.

a total of 397 ships lost, totalling some 2 million tons. The Americans were slow to respond, but eventually put an efficient convoy protection system in place which reduced the losses immensely.

Date:.........................January 13, 1942
Participants: ....Five U-boats under the command of Admiral Dönitz
Location of event:......The East Coast of the U.S.
Outcome: ....A total of 397 Allied ships lost, totalling some 2 million tons

Prisoners in the concentration camp at Sachsenhausen, Germany.

JANUARY 20, 1942

In 1941, Hitler ordered the physical extermination of the Jews—this was to be called "The Final Solution." SS chiefs Reinhard Heydrich and Adolf Eichmann were tasked with implementing this new wave of atrocities. Instead of permitting Jews to emigrate, they were to be shipped to far-away concentration camps where they would be killed in special killing centers.

The Final Solution needed the complicity of many leading Nazis, and to ensure that they all toed the line Heydrich and Eichmann organized the Wannsee Conference in 1942. Wannsee was a plush suburb of Berlin, and was a most unlikely setting for a meeting that was intended to co-ordinate the killing of 11 million innocent people. It was entitled the "Final Solution to the Jewish Question," and it gained the support of all those who attended.

Officially the Jews were told that they were being resettled in the east—this was not only to keep them from panicking and trying to escape, but it also ensured the support of the common German people. Fake propaganda films were made showing the Jews being moved into comfortable homes and enjoying their new lifestyle, and so little resistance was expressed.

The Jews were told to take their belongings and wait at predetermined locations to join a train. Once there, they were put into over-crowded boxcars, with no food, water or toilets. If this was not bad enough, the trains did not stop for several days, and large numbers of people died from starvation, dehydration and illness. Eichmann was responsible for the transportation of many millions of people—these included not just Jews but also Poles, Czechs, Russians, Gypsies,

As well as concentration camps there were many slave labour camps throughout Hitler's empire—locations where the enslaved populations of mainly eastern Europe were forced to work until they died.

These are slave laborers in the Buchenwald concentration camp near Jena; many had died from malnutrition when U.S. troops of the 80th Division entered the camp.

Communists and other "undesirables." Apart from those killed in the gas "ovens," deaths in the camps also occurred as the result of malnutrition, disease and beatings right up to the end of the war.

Date:	January 20, 1942
Participants:	Reinhard Heydrich, Heinrich Muller, Adolf Eichmann, Roland Friesler, and others
Location of event:	The Wannsee suburb of Berlin
Outcome:	The establishment of several extermination camps, including Belzec, Sobibor, Treblinka, and Majdanek, and the subsequent deaths of 11 million innocent people

US Forces arrive in London, England.

January 26, 1942

When Japan suddenly attacked Pearl Harbor, Hawaii, on December 7, 1941, America was pushed into finally joining the war. Soon afterward, British and American leaders got together and agreed that the European theatre should be considered a major priority.

General Marshall—a leading voice in the U.S. Army—wanted to build up American forces in Great Britain as soon as possible, and then launch a full-scale invasion on the Continent in 1943. Unfortunately, this was not a practicable solution—at this stage there were 37 U.S. Army divisions being trained and only one had completed its training and was in a position to go. The first of these U.S. ground troops arrived on British shores on January 26, 1942. However, they were not battle-ready, and did not go into action for the best part of a year. One of the secondary problems was that there were not enough ships to transport the numbers of soldiers that were needed across the Atlantic Ocean. American aircraft were prepared for combat sooner than the land forces, and participated in Allied raids on the Germans on July 4, 1942.

The lack of American troops in Great Britain was not a big issue at this point in the war—the British military commanders knew all too well how matters had progressed in northern France in World War I. They did not want to end up in a similar situation, with huge armies bogged down in mud-filled trenches fighting costly battles over a few feet of ground. Instead, they wanted to pursue the war in the Mediterranean until such time as an invincible invasion force could be assembled to take western Europe by storm. After much debate, President Roosevelt agreed, and instructed General Marshall to organize amphibious landings on the coast of North Africa so that U.S. forces could attack Rommel's Afrika Korps from the west and help bring the African campaign to a rapid close.

Date:..........................January 26, 1942
Participants: .............U.S. 34th Division
Location of event:......Great Britain
Outcome: ....The start of the build-up to the Allied invasion of mainland
Europe

FEBRUARY 27, 1942

The Battle of the Java Sea came about when an Allied naval force of combined Dutch, British, American and Australian ships intercepted a Japanese expedition convoy of transport ships which were on their way to stage an invasion of Java. The Japanese were well protected by warships as well as by a large contingent of aircraft. The first contact between the Allies and the Japanese occurred at just after 4pm on February 27, 1942, when the overall commander of the Allied force, Dutch Rear-Admiral Karel Doorman in the Dutch cruiser De Ruyter, ordered his flotilla to open fire. The Japanese fired back, and then tried to mount a torpedo attack. Under heavy Allied fire this failed and at least one Japanese destroyer was hit. A second Japanese destroyer flotilla then entered the battle from the opposite direction and managed to sink a Dutch destroyer with a long-range torpedo. The Royal Navy cruiser HMS Exeter was hit and unable to keep up, retiring from the conflict with a damaged boiler room.

The Allied vessels were then ordered to make a counter-attack, and a second round of fighting began. The Japanese tried to hide behind a smoke screen, but HMS Electra sailed straight through the smoke and engaged the enemy at close range, causing a large amount of damage to several vessels before being sunk with the loss of all but 54 hands. The Japanese then made use of the failing light to withdraw.

Japanese Mogame class cruiser in flames.

The commanders of the Allied flotilla spent the rest of the night trying to find the enemy, and there were several fierce engagements. During the night several Allied ships were sunk by Japanese torpedoes, and much damage was done on both sides by the sustained gunfire. On February 28, two Allied cruisers, HMAS Perth and USS Houston, ran unexpectedly into a second Japanese invasion fleet, and engaged it immediately. They successfully destroyed most of the transport vessels, but as they ran short of ammunition around 90 long-range torpedoes were launched at them by the Japanese covering force. They eventually sank—still firing their guns—with a great loss of life.

Date:......................February 27, 1942
Participants:................A large Japanese expedition of transports protected by
warships including the cruisers Nachi and Haguro
Eastern Strike Force under Dutch Rear-Admiral Karel
Doorman, including the cruisers De Ruyter and Java, and
destroyers Witte de With and Kortenaer
British China Force plus the Royal Navy cruiser HMS Exeter
and destroyers HMSs Jupiter, Electra, and Encounter
The heavy cruiser USS Houston, the Flagship of the U.S.
Asiatic Fleet
HMAS Perth under Captain H.M.L. Waller, DSO and Bar
Location of event:......Java Sea
Outcome:.................Much of the Allied fleet in the East Indies was destroyed

Orders in hand, Capt. Marc A. Mitscher, U.S.N., skipper of the U.S.S. Hornet (CU-8) chats with Maj. Gen. James Doolittle, U.S. Army. Some of the 80 Army fliers who took part in the historic Japanese raid are pictured.

The morale of the Allied public was low in the spring of 1942, and military commanders were anxious to do what they could to generate some good news for home consumption. When it was realized that army twin-engined bombers could successfully take off from an aircraft carrier, it was decided to launch a small bombing raid on the Japanese mainland. While this would do little significant damage to the targets, it was hoped that the news would boost the domestic situation.

The leader of the U.S. Army Air Forces, General Henry H. Arnold, chose Lieutenant Colonel James H. Doolittle to lead the raid. Under conditions of extreme secrecy, the talented colonel trained a small band of volunteer air crews for the mission. The plan was to use B-25B Mitchell medium bombers, taking off from the U.S. aircraft carrier Hornet when they were 400 miles off the coast of Japan. They would then fly over to Tokyo, where they would stage their bombing runs, and then continue on to the Chinese mainland.

In the event the raid began badly—on the morning of April 18, 1942, whilst still 600 miles off the coast of Japan, they were spotted by shipping and subsequent radio broadcasts warned of the American presence. Rather than abandon the mission, Doolittle ordered his men into the air, and the bombing raid went ahead. Sixteen B-25B Mitchells, each flown by a five-man crew, went into the attack and dropped their bombs on Tokyo and surrounding towns. None of the aircraft made it to the safety of Chinese airfields, but most of the men survived; three were executed by the Japanese after being taken prisoner.

Although the bomb damage was insignificant, it was a major embarrassment to the Japanese High Command, which resolved to

Army Lieut. Col. James H. Doolittle, taking off from USS Hornet (CV 8), Capt. Marc A. Mitscher commanding, bombed Tokyo, the first American air strike against the Japanese homeland. Hornet's mission was kept an official secret for a year; until then President Roosevelt referred to the origin of the Tokyo raid only as "Shangri-La."

destroy the Americans' ability to launch such raids in the future by sinking the U.S. aircraft carriers. This led to the decision to launch the offensive which resulted in the disastrous Battle of Midway, where the core of the Japanese navy was destroyed.

Date:	April 18, 1942
Participants:	Lieutenant Colonel James H. Doolittle and 16 B-25B Mitchell medium bombers U.S. aircraft carrier Hornet
Location of event:	Tokyo, Japan
Outcome:	The raid caused major embarrassment to the Japanese High Command—this led to their defeat at the Battle of Midway when they tried to sink U.S. aircraft carriers to prevent future raids

The Battle of the Coral Sea. U.S. carrier forces stopped a Japanese attempt to land at Port Moresby by turning back the covering carrier force. In the battle, the japanese lost the light carrier Shoho and the U.S. lost the carrier, USS Lexington (CV 2).

MAY 7–8, 1942

The Battle of the Coral Sea played an important part in the lead up to the great naval action at Midway, and as such is much more significant than may appear at first glance. It all started when the Japanese sent a large amphibious invasion force to take the strategically important town of Port Moresby, on the southeastern coast of New Guinea. To the Allies, a successful invasion would be a disaster—if the Japanese managed to establish an air-base in the area, it would not only threaten Allied shipping in the region but it would mean that air raids could be launched against the Australian mainland.

The Japanese invasion force was backed up by two big aircraft carriers—the Shokaku and the Zuikaku—along with their escorting cruisers and destroyers. The Allies—through their code-breaking activities—knew all about the Japanese fleet, and sent a large force of their own to attack it. This was composed of two of their own aircraft carriers, as well as several cruisers, destroyers, and submarines. They were supported by land-based bombers and patrol seaplanes.

When the two sides clashed on May 3-6, 1942 the exchange of fire cost the Allies one U.S. aircraft carrier, a destroyer and a vital fuel tanker; the second carrier was also damaged. The Japanese in comparison only lost a light carrier, one destroyer and a few smaller ships. While the Allied losses were heavier than those of their opponents, the battle was worthwhile from a strategic perspective. Not only did it force the Japanese to cancel their invasion plans but both of their aircraft carriers were damaged, and as a result had to return to port for major repairs. This meant that these vital vessels were unable to take part in the battle at Midway, which seriously weakened the overall Japanese naval capability.

Planes ready to take off from the deck of the USS Yorktown, during the Battle of the Coral Sea.

Date: .... May 7–8, 1942
Participants: .... A large Japanese fleet including the aircraft carriers Shokaku, Zuikaku, and Shoho as well as the Myoko, Haguro, Aoba, Furutaka, Kako, Kinugasa, and seven destroyers.
A large Allied fleet including the USSs Lexington, Yorktown, Hammann, Phelps, Minneapolis, New Orleans, Astoria, Chester, Australia, Chicago, Portland, Hobart, and 11 destroyers.
Location of event: ...... Coral Sea—southwest of the Solomon Islands and east of New Guinea.
Outcome: .... The Japanese plans to invade Port Moresby were cancelled and their largest aircraft carriers damaged, taking them out of service during the Battle of Midway.

The Reichsprotektor of Bohemia and Moravia, Reinhard Heydrich, in Prague in 1941.

MAY 27–JUNE 10, 1942

Reinhard Tristan Eugen Heydrich was born on March 7, 1904, into a well-off, but strongly anti-Semitic, Catholic family. In the early 1930s he came to the attention of Himmler, who was looking for someone to set up a counter-intelligence branch of the SS. Heydrich was given the job, and soon proved to be brilliant in his work, using his cold, calculating mind to invent new methods of trapping, humiliating, and destroying his enemies. His work was so important to the Nazis that he was promoted to the rank of SS Major within the year, and again to SS Colonel a year later. His counter-intelligence service was renamed as the Security Service—SD or Sicherheitsdienst—which included the Gestapo.

Heydrich built the Gestapo into a massive organization; its methods were extreme, and even minor infractions such as anti-Hitler jokes resulted in death sentences. Members of the Gestapo could arrest or murder anyone they wanted, and this instilled a reign of fear that spread throughout Germany. He did favors for Hitler, and his reputation was such that he became known as "The Blonde Beast" and as "Himmler's evil genius."

After Heydrich's assassination there were widespread reprisals but none so terrible than the destruction of Lidice where 172 men and boys over 16 were murdered by Nazi troops. This is a postwar remembrance service for the inhabitants of Lidice.

When the German armies invaded Russia in 1941, Heydrich was responsible for running special killing units called Einsatzgruppen. These units would go to Jewish villages and murder vast numbers of innocent civilians, usually by single shots to the back of the head. By the end of 1941, it was estimated that in the territory from the Ukraine to Latvia, Estonia, and Lithuania, almost half a million people had been massacred. When Heydrich was sent into Czechoslovakia to oversee the situation there, he quickly became known as "The Butcher of Prague" for his barbarous actions. In desperation, the exiled Czech government had two specially trained men parachuted into Czechoslovakia, where, with help from the partisans, in May 1942, they managed to inflict fatal injuries on Heydrich with a grenade.

After Heydrich died an elaborate funeral was staged for him in Berlin, and a furious Hitler ordered massive reprisals to be made on the local civilian population. The town of Lidice was used as an example to the Czech people, and almost the entire population there was liquidated.

Dates: ....May 27, 1942—Reinhard Heydrich attacked in Prague
June 4, 1942—Heydrich dies of wounds
June 10, 1942—Nazis liquidate Lidice in reprisal for the assassination
Participants: ....British-trained Czech resistance; Heydrich in dark green Mercedes
Location of event:......Kirchmayerstrasse, Prague
Outcome: ....Kaltenbrunner takes over as head of Security Police; Kurt Daluege takes over in Czechoslovakia and destroys Lidice

A payload of bombs is dropped over France.

MAY 30, 1942

In early 1942, one of Churchill's over-riding concerns was to ensure that the world saw Great Britain and her allies striking back hard at their Nazi aggressors. Air Marshal Arthur Harris, head of Bomber Command, was also an advocate of this policy, and with Churchill's encouragement decided to launch a major demonstration of Allied air power. This was code-named Operation "Millennium," and involved a thousand British-built and -piloted bombers making a devastating assault on a German target. Due to bad weather, the choice of destinations was limited, and the forecast dictated which would be the best option. In the end Cologne was chosen—it was an important city situated on the River Rhine, with a major armaments manufacturing center, and the site of an important railway junction. It was therefore of great strategic significance. Being such an important center, it was heavily defended, and a successful raid would have a great impact on the morale of the German populace.

The key to the raid would be to saturate the German defenses by putting so many aircraft over the target in such a short space of time that they would not be able to cope. Air Marshal Harris therefore used every aircraft he could lay his hands on, and the attack took place on a moonlit night on May 30, 1942. In all, he managed to assemble 1,047 bombers, which attacked the city in a relentless bombardment that lasted around two hours. In total they dropped 1,455 tons of bombs, two-thirds of which were incendiaries. The cost to the British was 39 aircraft missing—this amounted to a 3.3% casualty rate, which was less than expected, since the average was 4.6%.

RAF Bomber flies over Europe, bombing key German defences during operation "Millennium".

The conclusion was that raids of this size did indeed saturate the enemy defenses—although German radar had been able to track individual aircraft, their antiaircraft guns could not cope with such large numbers of aircraft. In the aftermath, reconnaissance photographs showed that around 600 acres of the city had been completely destroyed. German assessments showed that only 300 houses escaped unscathed and Cologne had become a ghost city.

Date:.........................May 30, 1942
Participants: ....1,047 bombers from Bomber Command under Air Marshal
                Harris
Location of event:......Cologne
Outcome: ....600 acres of the city of Cologne was completely destroyed by
                1,455 tons of bombs at a cost of 39 Allied aircraft missing.
                The raid proved that large numbers of aircraft flying in close
                proximity saturated the German air defence system, and so
                this became a standard operating procedure

A Japanese Nakalima B5N "Kate" is cut down by anti-aircraft fire from the USS Yorktown.

JUNE 4–6, 1942

As a result of the Doolittle bombing raid on Tokyo, the Japanese were desperate to sink the Americans' aircraft carriers to remove any possibility of it happening again. At this time the Japanese fleet was superior to that of the United States, which had been run down over many years as a result of the economic depression of the 1920s and 30s. The Japanese naval commanders therefore felt confident that they could take on the Allies on the open seas and win.

The Japanese naval commander Admiral Isoroku Yamamoto decided to stage an assault on the American fleet at its small mid-Pacific base at the Midway atoll by drawing them out into the open and attacking them. After destroying the fleet, he planned to launch an invasion of the atoll's two small islands so that he could establish Japanese airbases there. These would allow Japan's air forces to range much further than was previously possible. Yamamoto believed that the Americans would respond too slowly and in insufficient strength to resist the might of his well-trained and -equipped aircraft carriers.

What the Japanese did not know, however, was that their opponents had managed to crack their communications codes, and therefore knew in advance exactly what they were up to. The American U.S. Pacific Fleet commander, Admiral Chester W. Nimitz, set up a powerful ambush, and on June 4, 1942, when the Japanese sailed in for the attack, the trap was sprung. The resulting assault by aircraft launched by the Americans was the start of the second great carrier battle of the war, and it cost the would-be invaders four aircraft carriers for the loss of only one American carrier. This changed the balance of power in the Pacific, and from then on the Japanese naval fleet was put under increasing pressure by the Allies.

Crew members of the USS Yorktown work hard to repair damage incurred at the Battle of Midway.

Date:	June 4–6, 1942
Participants:	Japanese Combined Fleet under Admiral Isoroku Yamamoto
	U.S. Pacific Fleet under Admiral Chester W. Nimitz
Location of event:	Midway Atoll
Outcome:	Four Japanese aircraft carriers lost, to one American.

Torpedoed Japanese destroyer photographed through periscope of U.S.S. Wahoo or U.S.S. Nautilus, June 1942.

June 7, 1942

When the Japanese were making their plans to attack the U.S. base at Midway, they decided to stage an assault elsewhere to draw Americans forces out into the open. The target of this feint operation was the small island of Attu. This is the westernmost of the Aleutian Islands, and lies almost 1,100 miles from the mainland of Alaska and about 750 miles northeast of the Japanese Kurile Islands. Although the island was of little strategic importance, there was the possibility that long-range bombers could use it as a staging post for raids on the Canadian mainland. The Japanese had a naval base at Paramushiro Island, which lay only 650 miles southwest of Attu, and this was used as a launching point for the invasion.

When the Japanese mounted their invasion, the Americans were initially not expecting the attack. However, their code-breakers soon discovered the plan and the reasoning behind it. Since there was insufficient time to organize a proper defense, the Americans left the Japanese to their own devices until such a time as they were ready to clear the island on their own terms.

When they landed, the Japanese captured the only inhabitants, who had long suspected that they would one day be invaded. There were 41 native Attuans, and an American schoolteacher and his wife present on the day. In order to prevent other Aleutian islanders from being taken prisoner, the Americans evacuated 881 Aleuts with little more than a suitcase each, and then burned their homes to the ground to avoid them falling into enemy hands. They were then transported to southeast Alaska and housed in appalling conditions for the duration of the war. In many ways they were treated worse than if they had been prisoners of war, and many died of diseases such as pneumonia and tuberculosis.

Naval Air Station Attu (Casco Field), Aleutians, Alaska.

*The aft end of Enterprise's island showing the base of her aircraft crane and both 1.1"
antiaircraft gun mounts doing some target practice.*

Date:..........................June 7, 1942
Participants: ....Japanese 301st Independent Infantry Battalion
Location of event:......Attu, Aleutian Islands
Outcome: ....Japanese successfully invaded Attu; the forced evacuation
                        and subsequent mistreatment of the other islanders by their
                        "rescuers"

British artillery bombardment - start of counter attack at night.

JULY 1–30, 1942

The North African situation looked bleak for the British and Commonwealth forces in the summer of 1942. Although the Allies had managed to hold on to Egypt, the Afrika Korps looked ready to smash through the defensive lines and sweep across Egypt toward Alexandria and Cairo. Beyond this lay the vital Middle Eastern oilfields.

To maximize their chances of resisting German advances, British commanders made full use of the local topography. The Mediterranean Sea lay to the north and the Qattara Depression stretched across a vast area to the south. This was effectively a sand sea, and was more or less impassable to anything other than camels. The narrowest point between was a 40-mile gap, in which lay the settlement of El Alamein. The area had been fortified as fully as time and circumstances had allowed; however, this did not stop Rommel attacking on July 1. The Axis troops managed to break through the Allied defenses near El Alamein, but the battle took so long that the attack stalled. The next day Rommel attacked again, but Allied counter-attacks forced him to pull back and regroup.

Over the course of the month of July the battle front moved back and forth as both sides made gains and suffered losses. Although the good visibility offered by the desert environment was ideal for the Germans to exploit their superior antitank weaponry, it was also good ground for the British long-range artillery, and this proved to be a major asset for the Allies.

By July 31 the Axis advance on Alexandria and Cairo had been stopped, and the Allies ended offensive operations in order to allow their exhausted troops to rest. A major Axis counter-attack was expected, so the defensive line was considerably strengthened.

El Alamein - British troops pass an Italian M13-40 tank.

New Zealanders with prisoners they have rounded up.

Date:.........................July 1–30, 1942.
Participants: ....Allied Eighth Army under General Claude Auchinleck
German-Italian Afrika Korps led by Erwin Rommel
Location of event:......El Alamein
Outcome: ....The Axis advance on Cairo was halted

Three young Panzergrenadier soldiers in Sevastopol.

July 3–5, 1942

In October 1941, the German Army backed by two divisions of Romanian troops laid siege to the city of Sevastopol. Its defenders, however, put up a determined resistance, and held out against continued attacks. Hitler grew increasingly impatient for its capture as the city had great strategic significance, being the main Soviet naval port on the Black Sea. The Black Sea Fleet did its best to supply the city—despite its heroic efforts, however, the Soviet units holding the city were badly out-numbered and low on food, ammunition and equipment.

The Soviets' philosophy was that, although the loss of Sevastopol was considered inevitable, they would exploit the siege to draw as many Axis troops away from the rest of the battle-front for as long as possible. The city itself was one of the strongest fortress cities in the world, with three separate lines of defense which included minefields, wide antitank ditches, concrete bunkers and machine-gun nests. On top of this, the defenders had the awesome firepower of a heavily armed battleship and a destroyer which were both moored in the port, along with various smaller vessels.

In July 1942, Hitler launched Operation "Sturgeon"—the code-name for the final assault designed to break the inhabitants' last remaining defenses. His field commander was General von Manstein, who had put together an enormous assault force to take the city. It included 208 batteries of artillery and a huge railway gun which fired 9-ton armor-piercing or 5-ton high-explosive shells. After five days of continuous bombardment from both land and air, the Germans attacked. The Soviets put up a fierce resistance, and every fort, emplacement or building was defended to the last man. One by one, however, they fell and on July 3, 1942 the city was taken. In all, Sevastopol had held out for 250 days, and its loss signalled the end of Soviet resistance in the Crimea.

A German heavy mortar fires against Soviet forces.

A German anti-tank crew at Sevastopol. Munitions supply was extremely slow and German forces relied increasingly on capturing Soviet guns and ammunition.

Dates:	July 3, 1942—Germans take Sevastopol
	July 5, 1942—Soviet resistance in the Crimea ends.
Participants:	Soviet Black Sea Fleet, including the battleship Parishskaya Kommuna
	Soviet garrison of 7 infantry divisions and 3 marine brigades under the command of Admiral Yumashev
	Germans under General von Manstein had 7 divisions, their Romanian allies had 2 divisions
Location of event:	Sevastopol, Crimea
Outcome:	The Soviets lost their main port on the Black Sea, a major strategic blow

US landing craft on beach ; truck prepares to offload.

AUGUST 7, 1942

When 14,500 U.S. Marines landed on the islands of Guadalcanal and nearby Tulagi on August 7, 1942, it was the first stage in the Allied plan to retake the Solomon Islands from the Japanese invaders. It was also the first major Allied land offensive of the Pacific war. The assault was backed up by 82 warships and transports. These included the aircraft carriers Saratoga, Enterprise and Wasp, as well as the battleship USS North Carolina. The overall commander of the operation was Vice Admiral Robert. L. Ghormley, Commander-in-Chief of the South-Pacific Area.

The early morning attack was preceded by an intensive barrage of gunfire from the escort warships—this was designed to ensure that the Japanese base was unable to pose a threat to the troops landing nearby. The Japanese also had a naval base at Tulagi, and this was attacked by 16 F-4F Grumman Wildcat fighters—they managed to destroy seven Kawanishi military flying boats and eight Mitsubishi floatplanes. The Marines who landed on Guadalcanal met no opposition from the Japanese soldiers who had all run away into the jungle. On Tulagi, however, they met fierce resistance and took heavy casualties.

The Allied plan had been put into action very quickly, and as a result certain factors had not been thought through properly. The reason for the haste was that a new Japanese airbase had been under construction on Guadalcanal and the Allies desperately wanted to seize it before it could be made operational. Capturing and securing the new airfield was therefore the main priority of the invasion force; however, the problem was that it was well within range of Japanese bombers and warships.

US Marines wade up Tenaru River led by native guides.

The Japanese responded with several air raids, but covert ground observers were able to give advance warning of the attacks, and many of the aircraft were shot down by antiaircraft fire and waiting American fighter aircraft. As a result, little damage was done. The Japanese then tried to retake the airfield using ground troops, but after heavy fighting U.S. Marines and paratroops managed to stave them off. The ground war then continued for several months until the island of Guadalcanal was free of enemy soldiers.

Date: .... August 7, 1942
Participants: .... 1st U.S. Marine Division
Location of event: ...... Guadalcanal, Solomon Islands
Outcome: .... The liberation of Guadalcanal and the capture of the
                              Japanese airbase

The first big raid by the 8th Air Force was on a Focke Wulf plant at Marienburg. Coming back, the Germans were up in full force and we lost at least 80 ships-800 men, many of them pals.

AUGUST 17, 1942

The first USAAF headquarters were established at Daws Hill, High Wycombe, in February 1942, and then in June the Eighth Air Force headquarters were set up in Bushy Park, London. From these locations plans were put in place for U.S. aircraft to enter the war against Germany in Europe. The first bombing raids conducted by American aircraft were made in conjunction with British bombers, but on August 17, 1942, the 97th Bomb Group made the first U.S. heavy bomber raid over continental Europe.

In this attack 12 Boeing B-17 Flying Fortresses led by Colonel Armstrong attacked a major communications center to help disrupt the German war effort. The main targets were the Rouen-Sotteville railroad yards at Rouen, France, but at the same time six other B-17s created a diversion by flying along the Channel coast of northern France. Although this was only a small-scale operation, the targets were badly damaged and Colonel Armstrong was awarded the British Flying Cross as well as the Silver Star with oak leaf cluster (as an addition to the Distinguished Flying Cross which he already held). While all the bombers which took part were American-built and American-flown aircraft, the escorts were British Spitfires, and with this protection no aircraft were lost.

After the success of the Rouen raid, B-17s continued to attack targets in German-held areas. However, it was found that without close fighter protection they were vulnerable to frontal attack. On September 6, 1942, two B-17s were shot down by Luftwaffe fighters, and as a result of this

The crew of the celebrated "Memphis Belle".

15th Air Force, 455th Bomb Group, 742nd Bomb Squadron 16 High Altitude Missions WWII, European Theatre.

weakness and the numbers of aircraft being diverted to North Africa the B-17s flew only 27 missions in 1942. In August 1943, the B-17s were re-equipped with power-driven nose turrets which allowed the forward gunners to track enemy aircraft far more effectively. By this time the Consolidated B-24 Liberator had arrived in large numbers and German targets were subjected to relentless bombardments.

Date:........................August 17, 1942
Participants: ....97th Bomb Group protected by RAF Spitfires
Location of event:......The Rouen-Sotteville railroad yards at Rouen, France
Outcome: ....Lessons were learned by the USAAF and changes were made to tactics and equipment to reduce aircraft losses

Canadian troops with a Bren carrier vehicle, wait for their landing craft to take them into Dieppe.

AUGUST 19, 1942

In early 1942, the Axis powers were in a very strong position throughout Europe and northern Africa. Meanwhile, Churchill was anxious to test German defenses along the French coast to see how difficult it would be to launch a Continental invasion. Accordingly, a major raid was planned, and the French port of Dieppe chosen as the target. The raid, which was scheduled for July 1942, was given the code-name Operation "Rutter," and in preparation troops of the 2nd Canadian Infantry Division were sent for intensive training in amphibious operations.

The weather of July 1942 proved to be completely unsuitable, and so the raid was postponed. When it was resurrected, it was re-named Operation "Jubilee," and better weather allowed it to go ahead on the new date of August 19, 1942. Of the raiders, 4,963 were Canadian troops, 50 were American Rangers and 1,050 were British Commandos. In addition, there were eight Allied destroyers and 74 Allied air squadrons, eight of which belonged to the RCAF.

Whilst travelling toward their target, things started to go badly wrong when they ran into a small German naval convoy, and the exchange of gunfire alerted the coastal batteries, removing all chance of a surprise landing on the first sites. The British Commandos, who were tasked with the destruction of the coastal batteries at Berneval, were largely dispersed by the skirmish and therefore unable to provide effective support for the assault. Those who attacked the Varengeville battery, however, accomplished their task and successfully destroyed it. The Canadians, who were assigned to the attack on the port of Dieppe, as well as at Pourville just to the west, and at Puys to the east, fared very badly. They had lost the element of surprise as well as the cover of darkness, and

German soldier heavily laden with stick grenades inspects the destruction of the Dieppe beaches.

British commandos remain defiant following the Dieppe raid.

took very heavy casualties. Under very heavy fire many were successfully evacuated, although those who were left behind soon ran out of ammunition and were forced to surrender.

The Royal Air Force lost 106 aircraft and the RCAF lost 13. Of the 4,963 Canadians who took part, 907 were killed, and only 2,210 returned to England; 1,946 prisoners of war were taken. In many ways the raid was a disaster; however, it is certain that far fewer casualties were experienced during the D-Day landings as a result of the lessons learned at Dieppe.

Date: ....August 19, 1942
Participants: ....4,963 Canadian troops
　　　　　　　　　　　50 American Rangers
　　　　　　　　　　　1,050 British Commandos
　　　　　　　　　　　8 Allied destroyers and 74 Allied air squadrons
Location of event: ......Dieppe, France
Outcome: ....Although the raid was a complete disaster, it provided many valuable lessons that helped Allied planners make the D-Day landings successful

Column of British army vehicles pass the wreckage of a German Junkers JU52 transport aircraft.

SEPTEMBER 2, 1942

After Rommel's first major offensive against the Allied defenses at El Alamein in North Africa had stalled in July 1942, a fresh attack was expected at any time. Luckily for the Allies, their code-breaking operations gave sufficient warning when the attack finally came on September 2, 1942. By this stage the British forces were being led by General Bernard Law Montgomery, and he told his men that Rommel was going to attempt an outflanking maneuver from the south.

The Axis troops wanted to take two key geographical features—these were the ridges at Alam Halfa and Ruweisat. Had they achieved this, it would have given them high ground from which their artillery could have controlled much of the area. A field gun of the day had a range of more than 10 miles, and so this would have been a major blow to the Allied position. Knowing that this was Rommel's intention gave Montgomery a significant advantage, and he positioned his Eighth Army in the best place to defend the ridges.

Although Churchill was forever pushing Montgomery to attack, Montgomery knew that this was a war that was controlled by the amount of supplies the army had available.

He therefore took no notice of the Prime Minister's demands and
waited until he had sufficient supplies. Since America had finally entered
the war, there were enormous amounts of equipment arriving, including
large numbers of aircraft and the fuel to keep them flying. This gave the
Allies total air superiority, which not only made a massive difference
to the battlefield but meant that Axis supplies could not get through.
Montgomery knew that he could afford to sit back and wait for the
enemy to attack—all the time that the Allies were building up supplies,
the Germans were running out of fuel and equipment.

When the Axis armor finally attacked at Alam Halfa on September 2,
it took a severe pounding from a well co-ordinated combination of Allied
artillery, armor and air support and was forced to retreat. The battle was
over by September 7.

Date:.........................September 2, 1942
Participants: ....Eighth Army under Field Marshal Bernard Montgomery
                        Afrika Korps under General Erwin Rommel
Location of event:......The ridges at Alam Halfa and Ruweisat
Outcome: ....The Axis troops were heavily beaten, and as a result lost a
                        large amount of equipment and used up valuable supplies
                        that it could not replace

German SS - Das Reish, Shurzen plates.

SEPTEMBER 13, 1942

After the German Army's long withdrawal from Moscow, from December 1941, under constant harassment from the Red Army, a strong defensive line was finally established some 200 miles back from the Germans' original positions. With the relative security of his army regained, Hitler set about building up his forces to make another push forward.

Although Hitler knew that his main attention should have been to capture the oilfields of the Caucasus, he was obsessed with the idea of taking Stalingrad, which lay on the banks of the Volga and Don rivers. The German successes in defeating the Red Army at Kharkov in May 1942 had given him a deceptive opinion of the strength of Russian troops. As a result of this, he badly misjudged the likely performance of his armies in the coming battles. He therefore launched two separate offensives that summer—one to take land in the Caucasus, and the other, in the form of the Sixth Army, to capture Stalingrad.

In their efforts to capture Stalingrad, Hitler's troops met with incredible resistance. Although the Germans entered the city on September 12, it was very well defended, and occupied by fanatical soldiers who would die rather than give ground. After realising that his armies were not going to have it all their way, Hitler kept pulling units away from his other fronts to bolster the plan, instead of backing off to regroup. This seriously weakened the chances of his other commanders completing their objectives, as they were left with few supplies and no fresh units to back up their weary troops.

German Junkers flies in supplies for ground forces.

In his haste, Hitler had used poor-quality foreign troops to defend the impossibly long German flanks. The Soviets quickly exploited this weakness by driving through them and cutting off the Sixth Army in November 1942—this left all of its 250,000 men completely encircled, and without hope of immediate relief. (See also page 114.)

Date:.........................September 13, 1942
Participants: ....Field Marshal von Brauchitsch, Commander-in-Chief of the Army, which was composed of 330,000 men of Army Group B including General Paulus's Sixth Army and Fourth Panzer Army as well as Romanian divisions
The Red Army, including: Marshal Georgi Zhukov and General Vasilevsky, the Sixty-second Army, commanded by General Vasily Ivanovich Chuikov
Location of event:......Stalingrad, Southeastern Soviet Union
Outcome: ....Hitler failed to take Stalingrad, and lost 330,000 men together with large quantities of equipment. This weakened the Wehrmacht so badly that it never recovered

The USS Enterprise following a hit from a Japanese bomber.

OCTOBER 25, 1942

The Battle of Santa Cruz involved the aircraft carriers of the Japanese and American navies in an action that started on October 25, 1942, and lasted for two days. It was fought to gain control of the seas off Guadalcanal, as this would give the winner access to the strategically important Henderson Field airbase recently constructed on the island.

The Japanese came into the battle with four aircraft carriers, four battleships, nine cruisers, twenty-eight destroyers, eleven submarines and seven other vessels. This was an enormous fighting force, and the U.S. had less than half the number of ships to fight back with.

The battle was waged by large numbers of aircraft which were launched in several waves—these did their best to bomb, torpedo or strafe the ships of the other side, and the damage exacted by them was considerable.

At the end of the battle, the Americans had lost the carrier Hornet, which was so badly damaged that it was abandoned. This represented a serious loss, and to make matters worse, the carrier Enterprise, while still afloat, was also in a very bad condition. The Imperial Japanese Navy for its part had all but run out of fuel, and was unable to continue the battle. It had also lost the bulk of the aircraft it had launched from its carriers:none had enough aircraft left to function. While these losses in themselves were considerable, the loss of hundreds of trained pilots was far more serious as they could not be replaced.

The Battle of Santa Cruz was tactical victory for the Japanese; however, it was a massive strategic defeat. The Americans still had the Henderson Field airbase, and although the Enterprise was damaged, it was still a very potent weapon. The battle also set the stage for the naval actions in the Battles of Guadalcanal in mid-November.

The USS Indiana opens fire.

Date:..........................October 25, 1942
Participants:..............The Japanese fleet consisted of:
4 aircraft carriers:the Shokaku, Zuikaku, Junyo, and Zuiho
4 battleships:Hiei, Kirishima, Kongo, and Haruna
9 cruisers; 28 destroyers; 11 submarines and 7 other ships
The American fleet consisted of:
USSs Enterprise, Hornet, South Dakota, Portland,
Northampton, Pensacola, Juneau, San Diego, San Juan, and
14 destroyers.
Location of event:......The seas off Guadalcanal
Outcome:..................The Japanese lost the bulk of the pilots from their carrier-
based air force. This considerably reduced their ability to
conduct operations in the area

British troops manning 6 lb guns in El Alamein.

NOVEMBER 1, 1942

After the Axis armies in North Africa had been beaten back at Alam Halfa in September 1942, General Montgomery ordered his men to fall back to the El Alamein defensive line, where they dug in and waited for the Germans to attack. By late summer 1942, the Afrika Korps was in a desperate situation—Allied air power had built up to the point where very few German supplies were getting through. In addition, British code-breaking activities revealed the whereabouts of Axis fleets, and very few ships reached their destinations. The vast distances that had to be covered in the North African campaign meant that fuel was a critical factor, and once Field Marshal Rommel's highly mechanized troops began to run dry, things got much worse.

Meanwhile, Montgomery continued to amass military stores. His philosophy was brutally simple—he would not attack until he had enough equipment to make sure that victory was certain. The massive quantities of hardware grew to the point where in mid-October 1942 he had 195,000 men, 1,900 pieces of artillery and 1,351 tanks, of which many were the new Sherman M4 and Grant M3 tanks. He was finally satisfied that the time for attack was right, and on October 23 he unleashed the largest artillery bombardment since World War I. Rommel was on sick leave in Austria at the time, and his stand-in, General George Stumme, collapsed and died of a heart-attack during the 1,000-gun barrage. Hitler ordered Rommel to return to Egypt immediately.

Montgomery then launched Operation "Supercharge" on November 1, 1942—this was a large-scale attack on the Afrika Korps at Kidney Ridge. When the Eighth Army broke through his lines, Rommel realized that he was going to be surrounded and signalled a general retreat. Large numbers of Axis troops were taken prisoner, and much valuable

A German shell explodes close to a British truck carrying infantry.

equipment was lost. Rommel's situation worsened still further when he was told that the U.S. Army, led by General Dwight D. Eisenhower, had landed in Tunisia, Morocco and Algeria on November 8, and was headed his way.

Date:	November 1, 1942
Participants:	General Erwin Rommel and the Afrika Korps
	Field Marshal Bernard Montgomery and the Eighth Army
Location of event:	El Alamein
Outcome:	Rommel lost a significant amount of men and equipment; this signaled the start of a long retreat westward which finally ended with the surrender of the Axis forces in North Africa

US troops come ashore at Arzan near the port of Oran and Casablanca.

NOVEMBER 8, 1942

The summer of 1942 was a difficult time for the Allies—no matter how badly they wanted to stage a landing on the European mainland, there was no real opportunity to do so. Russia, however, had been putting enormous pressure on the West to open a second front in order to draw German troops away from her borders. In July 1942, Franklin D. Roosevelt and Winston Churchill came to the conclusion that the best course of action would be to invade French-held northwest Africa.

General Dwight D. Eisenhower was put in charge of the invasion, which was given the code-name Operation "Torch." His troops faced over 100,000 Vichy-French soldiers who were spread across Algeria, Morocco and Tunisia. On November 8, 1942 Allied forces landed in Casablanca, Oran and Algiers. The Vichy-French troops at Oran fought back, and General Mark Clark wasted little time in trying to broker a peace deal with Admiral Jean-François Darlan, who was their Commander-in-Chief. Hitler was furious that Darlan was negotiating with the Americans instead of fighting them. He told Pétain that if his troops did not fight, German soldiers would annexe Vichy France. Darlan surrendered his forces on November 11, and an enraged Hitler lived up to his word.

The Allied invasion force continued to move eastward, and almost got to Tunis before meeting elements of the Afrika Korps. At this stage the rest of Rommel's army was being chased westward along the coast of North Africa by Montgomery and the Eighth Army. Before long the Axis

US troops in Operation "Torch" and their landing craft LCM(3).

army arrived in southern Tunisia with the Allied forces not far behind. Realising that a massive fight lay ahead of him, Montgomery once again decided to sit and wait for enough supplies to reach him before attacking. Rommel knew that the longer he waited, the stronger his opponent would be, so he pre-empted the Allies and struck out at the approaching Americans at the Faid and Kasserine Passes.

Date:.........................November 8, 1942
Participants: ....Operation commander:Dwight D. Eisenhower
Naval Commander-in-Chief, the Allied Expeditionary Force, Admiral Sir Andrew Cunningham, Bart, GCB
The Western Assault Force—Objective Casablanca in French Morocco
Maj Gen George S. Patton, 35,000 troops
Central Task Force—Objective Oran
Maj Gen Lloyd R. Fredendall, 18,500 troops building up to 39,000
Eastern Task Force—Objective Algiers
Lt Gen K.A.N. Anderson, 20,000 troops, half American and half British
Location of event:......Casablanca, Oran, and Algiers in Northwest Africa
Outcome: ....Rommel was caught from two sides by an overwhelmingly superior force

Loading bomb on SBD aboard USS Enterprise.

In November 1942, the Japanese once again returned to Guadalcanal with the intention of re-taking the Henderson Field airbase established by the Americans when they took the island in August of that year. They had by this stage realized that the American military presence on Guadalcanal was more than the small expeditionary force that their early assessments had indicated. They had also come to the conclusion that if they wanted to regain control of the seas in the region, they would first have to take the airbase back. In order to achieve this, they amassed thousands of troops and assembled a large convoy of merchant ships. These vessels had enough supplies to sustain a month-long ground battle.

The ground offensive would be preceded by a massive naval bombardment of the Henderson Field airbase, after which the troops would go in to finish the job. The Japanese warships that were due to deliver this massive artillery assault entered a small area of sea close to the airbase, known as Ironbottom Sound, at around 1.00am on the morning of November 13, 1942. When they arrived they discovered an American force of cruisers and destroyers waiting for them. A series of mishaps on both sides resulted in the ships engaging each other at ridiculously close range. Although the Americans came out of the encounter much the worse for wear, they succeeded in preventing the naval bombardment from taking place.

Since the American fleet was severely depleted by the battle, the American theatre commander, Admiral William Halsey, sent his fastest battleships to reinforce the area. Accompanied by four destroyers, they managed to reach Ironbottom Sound on November 14. Shortly after they arrived, a second Japanese force came on the scene, also intending to bombard the airbase. Just as the enemy ships approached, the USS

A Japanese dive bomber shot down over USS Enterprise.

South Dakota lost electrical power and came under heavy fire. Although not severely damaged, she nevertheless took a lot of hits. Meanwhile, the commander of the USS Washington managed to get close to the enemy fleet without being seen, and with the aid of some superb gunnery control blew the lead Japanese ship, the Kirishima, out of the water. She then sank the Ayanami in short order, all the while managing to avoid several torpedo attacks.

The three-day naval battles of Guadalcanal marked a turning point in the Pacific war. In all, the Japanese lost two battleships, one heavy cruiser, three destroyers and eleven combat transports, as well as 5,000 troops and several thousand sailors killed. These were losses they could not sustain; thereafter they continued to be pushed back across the Pacific until the end of the war.

Date:..........................November 12–15, 1942
Participants: ..............U.S. fleet consisted of: Task Force 67 under Rear Admiral Richmond Kelly Turner with 4 transport ships, 20 cruisers, and destroyers. Task Force 16 under Rear Admiral Thomas C. Kinkaid with the carrier USS Enterprise with Air Group 10 and 8 cruisers and destroyers. Task Force 64 under Rear Admiral Willis A. Lee with 2 battleships and 2 destroyers. Task Force 63 under Rear Admiral Aubery W. Fitch with the Cactus Air Force and Marine Air Groups 14 and 25
The Japanese combined fleet under Admiral Isoroku Yamamoto; the Advance Force under Vice-Admiral Nobutake Kondo with 2 battleships, 20 destroyers and cruisers. The Carrier Support Group under Vice-Admiral Takeo Kurita with 2 carriers, 2 battleships, and several destroyers. The Outer Seas Forces under Vice Admiral Gunichi Mikawa C–in–C Eighth Fleet with 12 destroyers and cruisers. The Reinforcement Group under Rear-Admiral Raizo Tanaka with 11 destroyers and 12 transport ships
Location of event:......The seas around Guadalcanal
Outcome: ....The Japanese lost so many vessels that they were unable to hold back Allied forces; they never recovered and were continually pushed back toward Japan

Pocket Battleship Lutzow firing its guns.

DECEMBER 31ST, 1942

The Battle of the Barents Sea was, in itself, not particularly remarkable as a naval action. At the end of December 1942, an Allied Arctic convoy, much like many that had gone before it, was attacked by German vessels. Composed of merchant ships escorted by a small contingent of the Royal Navy, it was making its way to deliver supplies to the Russian port of Murmansk.

The convoy itself was made up of 14 merchant ships and tankers, which together carried around 200 tanks, 2,500 trucks, 125 aircraft, 18,000 tons of fuel oil, 13,000 tons of aviation fuel and 54,000 tons of other military equipment. The escorted was composed of six British destroyers under the command of Captain Robert St. V. Sherbrooke.

What makes the battle so significant, however, is that it had consequences that far outreached the day's events. For many years Hitler had berated the German Naval Command for being inept, timid and poorly motivated, asserting that it was a breeding ground for revolutionaries and a poor imitation of the British navy. He admired the U-boat fleet under the command of Admiral Dönitz for its daring and the magnificent results it had delivered, but the surface fleet was another matter. At the end of 1942, two of Hitler's armies were besieged at Stalingrad, and he was very concerned about the amount of supplies that the Allies were delivering to the Soviets through the Barents Sea. He therefore ordered Admiral Kübler, who was the commander in charge of his northern sector, that he should attack the enemy vigorously, but with great caution. This conflicting order put Kübler in an impossible position, although he did his best to obey it.

German heavy cruiser "Admiral Von Hipper".

Kübler's plans were code-named Operation "Regenbogen" (Rainbow), and to implement them he had the pocket-battleship Lützow and the heavy cruiser Hipper, with an escort of six destroyers. They soon sighted the Allied fleet, and gunfire was quickly exchanged. The destroyer Achates was badly damaged, but managed to get the surviving crew off before she sank. Determined action by the British fleet harassed the Hipper, such that she was damaged and turned away without reaching the convoy. The Lützow managed to get very close to the merchant ships and fired 87 11-inch and 75 6-inch rounds. However, hampered by poor visibility, she failed to hit any of them and withdrew. The German destroyer Friedrich Eckholdt was engaged by the British, and she sank within two minutes.

As a result of its failure to sink any of the Allied convoy, Hitler completely lost faith in his surface fleet, and ordered all the heavy vessels to be broken up for scrap. Admiral Raeder was replaced by Dönitz, who later managed to get a reprieve for some of the ships. None the less, the German surface fleet was considerably neutered as a result of the Battle of the Barents Sea.

Date: .... December 31, 1942
Participants: .... The Allied convoy consisted of:
14 merchant ships and tankers escorted by six British destroyers under Captain Robert St. V. Sherbrooke.
The German fleet consisted of:
pocket-battleship Lützow and the heavy cruiser Hipper, with an escort of six destroyers under Admiral Kübler
Location of event: ...... The Barents Sea
Outcome: .... Hitler lost any remaining faith he had in his surface navy, and threatened to have the entire fleet broken up for scrap. From this point on the German surface navy ceased to have a significant impact on the war

Girauld, Roosevelt, de Gaulle, Churchill.

JANUARY 14–24, 1943

In early 1943, from January 14 to January 24, a conference of historical significance between Winston Churchill and Franklin D. Roosevelt was held in Casablanca, Morocco. When it started, its aims were somewhat unclear, as the original intention was for Stalin to attend as well. The difficult situation back in the Soviet Union—with the country besieged by both Hitler and the harsh winter—meant that he was not able to attend.

When Franklin D. Roosevelt travelled to the conference, it was the first time that an American President had been to Africa, and the first time that one had ever left the country during a time of war. His trip was kept secret from the American public at the time although he and Churchill made a deliberate point of doing some tourist sightseeing in the medieval marketplace in Casablanca. This united front was for the benefit of German spies, so that they would report back to Hitler that their alliance was holding firm.

By the time the conference ended, the path had been laid for the manner in which the rest of the war would be conducted. More importantly than this, it also set out the terms for Germany's unconditional surrender. In doing so, the conference achieved several things. For a start, it demonstrated that both the British and Americans were determined to permanently eliminate the threat of Nazi Germany. This gave the Soviets great assurance, and helped them to keep on fighting on the eastern front. It also gave Hitler the clear message that he had no hope of brokering a peace deal—he and his Nazi government would have to fight to the bitter end. As a result of these factors, the conference was a great success, and it paved the way toward the final Allied victory in Europe..

Roosevelt & Eisenhower.

US Soldier on guard at the Casablanca conference.

Date:..........................January 14–24, 1943
Participants: ....Churchill and Roosevelt
Location of event:......Casablanca
Outcome: ....It set out the terms for Germany's unconditional surrender

Soviet KV-1 heavy tanks on outskirts of Stalingrad.

FEBRUARY 2, 1943

Hitler's underestimation of the strength of the Soviets sealed the fate of his Sixth Army at Stalingrad. Once it was encircled by the Red Army in November 1942 there was little the Germans could do about it. The only sensible option would have been to stage a breakout, but Hitler forbade any such idea—he'd captured Stalingrad and wasn't going to relinquish it without a fight. The Luftwaffe did its best to supply the beleaguered troops, but it lost so many aircraft to Soviet attacks that it simply could not feed so many mouths and equip so much military hardware with the aircraft available to it. As time went on, more and more airfields were lost to the advancing Red Army, and the situation deteriorated still further for the occupying soldiers. In addition, it was the middle of the Russian winter, and many troops succumbed to the extreme temperatures.

After six months of fighting, the main German force commanded by General Paulus was out of food and ammunition, and most of the men were in a terrible physical condition. Unable to continue the fight, the Germans surrendered on January 31, 1943. A small isolated pocket of troops held out for another two days, but then finally capitulated. In all, about 91,000 soldiers surrendered, including 24 generals. It is thought that a total of around 147,200 German troops were killed as a result of

Hitler's determination to hold on to the city. The defeat was a great shock to the German people, and it was proclaimed that there would be four days of national mourning.

The Germans' surrender at Stalingrad was their first significant defeat on the Eastern Front. They had been beaten by a combination of Hitler's blind refusal to listen to his officers and an underestimation of the strength and resolve of the Red Army. Nor had Hitler understood the vastness of the Russian geography and the ferocity of the weather when he first contemplated Operation "Barbarossa." Stalingrad marked a real turning point in the fortunes of the German armies, not just on the eastern front, but for the entire war effort.

Date:........................February 2, 1943
Participants: ....The Soviets:
                Seven armies commanded by Rokossovsky's Don Front, including the Sixty-fifth Army, Twenty-first Army and Chuikov's Sixty-second Army
                The Axis:
                Sixth Army under General Friedrich Paulus
                Field Marshal Erhard Milch was in charge of the air re-supply of Stalingrad
Location of event:......Stalingrad
Outcome: ....Germany proclaimed three days of national mourning; Soviet forces advanced on all fronts

The 2nd Battalion, 16th Infantry, march through the Kasserine Pass and on to Kasserine and Farriana, Tunisia. 26 Feb 1943.

FEBRUARY 14–25, 1943

When Rommel and his armies began their retreat from the British Eighth Army along the coast of North Africa after the Battle of El Alamein in November 1942, his main goal was to get closer to his main supply point at Tunis. When he finally reached his chosen destination he wasted little time in resupplying his troops. Knowing that Montgomery was building up his forces to attack, Rommel struck out at the first opportunity. He decided that his best target would be the inexperienced American troops approaching from the west, and so he led his Afrika Korps into battle against them at the Faid Pass in the Tunisian Dorsal Mountains on February 14, 1943.

When the Americans came face to face with Axis troops for the first time they experienced a rude awakening. They had been trained in out-of-date text book battlefield tactics, which when matched against Rommel's well-honed methods quickly left them in total disarray. They experienced heavy losses in both men and equipment, and soon fell back. When the American troops established fresh defenses, Rommel realized that the Kasserine Pass was their weak spot and on February 19 he attacked again. This time he killed around 1,000 American troops, took large numbers prisoner, and captured huge quantities of heavy equipment.

The American commanders learned by their mistakes, however, and the next time the opposing forces met it was Rommel who lost out. The most important lesson had been that massed firepower was the key to defeating armored Axis forces. The Americans quickly worked out how to combine concentrated artillery barrages with aircraft attacks. On February 23 they struck back by launching a massive air attack, and intense bombing drove Rommel back through the Kasserine Pass. The

General Bernard L. Montgomery watches his tanks move up.

Americans, however, failed to press home their advantage and allowed Rommel to reach his fortifications at the Mareth Line. This was a 22-mile-long defensive system that had originally been built by the French to defend Tunisia against the Italians. While it was a temporary safe haven, it was not long before Montgomery's Eighth Army arrived to bring a conclusion to the conflict.

Date:...........................February 14–25, 1943
Participants: ..............U.S. 1st Armored Division and German Panzers
Location of event:......Faid and Kasserine passes
Outcome: ....Despite early defeats, the Americans quickly learned how to cope with their Afrika Korps opponents by using closely combined artillery, aircraft, and troops

PT's patrolling off coast of New Guinea.

The large island of New Guinea, which lies just to the north of Australia, was in an enormously important strategic position. For the Japanese it was a vital stepping stone toward the invasion of Australia itself. Admiral Yamamoto was therefore determined not to relinquish his bases on the island, which had come under intense pressure from Allied ground troops. In order to reinforce his troops at their base at Lae, he assembled a large fleet to resupply them. This was made up of eight destroyers and eight transport ships, which in total carried around 6,000 fresh soldiers.

On February 28, 1943 the convoy sailed out of the fortress port of Rabaul and made for its destination of Lae, through the Bismarck Sea. The flotilla was spotted by a Royal Australian Air Force reconnaissance B-24 Liberator the next day—this confirmed reports from Allied code-breakers of the convoy's existence. It was recognized that, if the extra troops were able to reinforce those already on the ground, New Guinea would be lost.

Stopping the reinforcements arriving became a top priority for the Allies, and a raid by B-17 Flying Fortresses was quickly mounted. This managed to sink two of the transport ships, but the convoy continued on its way. The Allies therefore put together a large strike force to ensure that it did not get through. On March 3 this attacked with a total combined force of 97 Allied fighters and bombers. Sweeping in low, straight out of the morning sun, they managed to sink four of the eight Japanese destroyers, as well as all the remaining transport ships. A second force of 330 Allied aircraft then strafed the surviving troops—who by then were mostly clinging to wreckage—to ensure that they did not reach the shore. It is thought that about 3,000 died in this secondary action,

A PT marksman provides a striking camera study as he draws a bead with his 50 caliber machine gun on his boat off New Guinea.

which the Japanese call the "Bismarck Sea Massacre." The battle put an end to Japanese attempts to bolster their ground forces in New Guinea as well as spelling the end of their aspirations for the island.

Date: .... March 2–4, 1943
Participants: .... A convoy of 8 destroyers and 8 transport ships under Admiral Yamamoto
Aircraft from the RAAF and USAAF
Location of event: ...... The Bismarck Sea
Outcome: .... The loss of 8 Japanese transport ships, 4 destroyers, and the deaths of 3,000 troops

Coast Guardsmen on the deck of the U.S. Coast Guard Cutter Spencer watch the explosion of a depth charge which blasted a Nazi U-boat's hope of breaking into the center of a large convoy. Sinking of U-175.

MARCH 16-20, 1943

The Battle of the Atlantic was described by Winston Churchill as the longest campaign of World War II. It began when hostilities broke out in 1939, and ended only when Germany surrendered in 1945. For Churchill it was also the dominating factor throughout the war, since the survival of Britain and the successful implementation of an Allied landing in Europe depended to a large extent on getting supplies across the Atlantic.

Both the Allies and the Axis powers fought the battle using surface vessels, submarines, and aircraft. The Kriegsmarine's U-boats were the Germans' main weapon—these came into full play with the fall of France in 1940, when they were able use the French west coast Atlantic ports.

The Battle of the Atlantic can be considered to have had four separate phases. The first phase was from July 1940 to December 1941—this was when Great Britain was struggling alone against the German peril. The Germans' U-boats operated in large "wolf-packs," mercilessly sinking any British shipping they could find in night-time raids. The second phase, from when America finally joined the war in December 1941 until March 1943, was a period in which the U-boats continued to grow in strength, sinking a total of 7 million tons of merchant shipping. During this time the Allies worked furiously to try to develop countermeasures to fight back against the submarine attacks.

U-Boat 118 comes under Allied attack.

The climax of the Battle of the Atlantic is considered to be between March 16 and March 20, 1943, when 27 ships were lost to U-boats. After this, however, in the third phase between April and May 1943, the German submarines started to suffer from the Allies' improved defenses—improved air cover, improved convoy tactics and submarine detection aids. The U-boats took heavy losses and had to be temporarily withdrawn from service to be re-equipped. The fourth, and final, phase was when the Allies went on the offensive helped by British code-breaking activities, along with sonar and radar. They struck back and heavily defeated the U-boat menace. In all, the Battle of the Atlantic was fought at a terrible cost—2,753 Allied ships were sunk along with 785 Nazi U-boats.

Date:......................March 16–20, 1943
Participants: ....U-boats of the Kriegsmarine
                    Allied merchant and naval shipping
Location of event:......The Atlantic Ocean
Outcome: ....2,753 Allied ships lost against 785 Nazi U-boats

Soldiers unload landing craft on the beach at Massacre Bay, Attu, on 13 May 1943. LCVPs in the foreground are from Zeilin (APA-3) and Heywood (APA-6).

MAY 11–JUNE 30, 1943

When the Japanese invaded Attu Island in the Aleutians to try to draw the U.S. fleet out into the open, the American commanders knew all about the plan as a result of Allied code-breakers' warnings. Instead, they left the Japanese to hold what was seen as a strategically unimportant island until Allied forces were ready to expel them. When the time was right to attack the nearby Kurile Islands, however, it was deemed necessary to first remove the Japanese forces from Attu.

Attu's remote position meant that it was very difficult to resupply. When the Japanese tried to reinforce their garrisons in January 1943, the Allies managed to defeat the attempt and exacted heavy losses on the Japanese force. A large contingent of troops from the U.S. Army's 7th Division was landed on Attu in March 1943, and they quickly set about their task. After some 20 days of fierce fighting, the Japanese finally realized that all was lost, and they ended the battle with a massed, drunken "Banzai" charge. Their forces on the island were almost completely annihilated, and only 28 of the original 4,700 troops lived to tell the tale.

Shortly afterward, the American 10th Mountain Division together with a Canadian force landed on the nearby island of Kiska. They too experienced some fierce fighting, but one morning they found that the island had been abandoned under the cover of fog by all the Japanese forces—all, that is, except for a small holding contingent who then committed suicide.

The Aleutian Islands were then used as bases by American bombers which continuously attacked the Kurile Islands, which were Japan's northernmost outposts, right up until the end of the war.

Soldiers pull an ammunition cart along the beach at Massacre Bay, Attu, 12 May 1943. One of the LCVPs in the background is from Zeilin (APA-3).

Flying Boat at naval air station, Attu.

Date: .... May 11–June 30, 1943
Participants: .... U.S. 7th Division
Japanese Aleutian garrison
Location of event: ...... Attu, Aleutians Islands
Outcome: .... All but 28 of the 4,700 Japanese troops were killed. The
Allies established important airbases on the Aleutians

British Army Churchill tank moving through the desert during the battle of El Alamein. General Montgomery defeated 13 German and Italian Divisions, decisively altering the balance of power in North Africa in favour of the Allies.

MAY 13, 1943

The Axis troops in North Africa were in a poor state by the beginning of May 1943—their humiliating defeat at El Alamein had left them severely weakened, and their morale was very low. They lost a large proportion of their heavy equipment in the hasty retreat from El Alamein, and badly needed to regroup and resupply. Unfortunately for them, very few supplies were getting through—nearly all their ships were being sunk by Allied aircraft. This was as a result of British code-crackers finding out where and when the supply convoys were sailing. Rommel's vehicles were running out of fuel, and ammunition supplies were dangerously low. In addition, the Americans had put the U.S. II Corps under the command of Major General George S. Patton. His leadership helped the inexperienced troops become efficient soldiers.

In early April, Montgomery organized an assault on the Afrika Korps in conjunction with Patton's forces, with the Americans attacking from the west and his Eighth Army from the east. Unable to resist the massive forces before them, the Axis troops were relentlessly pushed back toward the coast, and the two Allied armies finally linked up on April 7. This left the entire Axis army—composed of German, Italian and a small number of French soldiers—squeezed into a tiny area in the northeastern tip of Tunisia.

On April 19 the final assault began, and by May 7 British tanks entered Tunis. The writing was on the wall for the Axis forces, and short of ammunition, fuel and food, they surrendered on May 13, 1943. Over 275,000 prisoners of war were taken by the Allies, and a major phase of World War II came to an end. The way was now open to begin preparations for an assault on the European mainland.

Company D, 18th Infantry, 1st Infantry Division, dug-in in the hills south of El Guettar, Tunisia, North Africa.

Date:	May 13, 1943
Participants:	Field Marshal Bernard Montgomery's Eighth Army
	Major General George S. Patton's U.S. II Corps
	Axis forces including the Afrika Korps
Location of event:	Tunis
Outcome:	The surrender of German forces in North Africa; the Allies were now free to launch their invasion of Italy

German anti-tank gun.

JULY 5, 1943

After the Germans' humiliating defeat at Stalingrad in February 1943, Hitler knew that it was only a matter of time before the Red Army would have grown in size and strength past the point at which he could hope to compete with it. He therefore decided to launch an offensive to smash the Soviets before it was too late. He threw the bulk of his heavyweight armor into a massive tank battle at Kursk, in an attempt to encircle a large part of the Red Army. Although his generals warned him that the Soviets knew of the plan, Hitler ignored them, and committed to the assault 3,000 tanks, including the latest models of Panthers and Tigers, as well as 1,800 tactical aircraft.

The plan was for two large German armies to move in a pincer formation to cut off a large part of the Red Army. This would involve the Ninth Army coming down from the north and the Fourth Panzer Army moving up from the south. The battle began on July 4, 1943, but by July 11 the Germans had lost momentum, and the Soviets mounted a strong counterattack. In the end it turned into a battle of attrition, as tanks fought one another in a massive confrontation. It was a tactic that the Germans simply could not win. In the short amount of time since the war had started, the Russian people had achieved an industrial feat of super-human proportions. They had not only relocated their factories from sites vulnerable to the advancing Germans to safety beyond the Ural Mountains, but they had worked them night and day manufacturing military equipment. The Red Army now had so many tanks that the technically superior German models were simply overwhelmed. The Soviet railway system became such a ceaseless conveyor belt of new tanks, aircraft and other hardware that victory for the Red Army became inevitable.

Russian troops engaged in combat.

German Panzer III tanks, at the Battle of Kursk.

When the Americans landed on Sicily on July 13, Hitler realized that he needed to ensure that he still had enough equipment to defend against an Allied landing in mainland Europe. He therefore ordered a withdrawal from Kursk, leaving behind 70,000 dead and nearly 3,000 wrecked tanks.

Date: ....July 4, 1943
Participants: ....The Ninth Army attacking from the north and the Fourth Panzer Army from the south
Location of event: ......Kursk, Russia
Outcome: ....Defeat for the Germans. It proved to be their last major eastern offensive

Landing ship tank off the coast of Sicily.

JULY 9–10, 1943

At the Casablanca Conference held in January 1943, the Allied leaders agreed that their next offensive would be against the island of Sicily, and that this would form the basis of an Allied invasion of the Italian mainland. Such a plan would establish another front in the battle to wear Hitler and his forces down, and provide an overland route toward the goal of invading Germany.

The island was attacked from two sides simultaneously, with Montgomery's British forces landing on the southeast coast while Patton's U.S. Seventh Army landed from the southwest. The Americans were tasked with capturing Axis airfields and protecting the flanks of the British troops as they drove across the island. To help bolster the two landing forces, a large number of airborne troops were also dropped, and although they missed their targets, they did manage to cause immense confusion by cutting communications lines. The landings went well, and the Germans took several hours to attack the Seventh Army's beachheads with armored forces. These were fought off by a combination of naval and artillery gunfire backed up by ground troops.

As the British tried to push forward, German units mounted a determined defense of the road to the Sicilian capital, Messina. Patton was then ordered to take Palermo at the western tip of the island, and then to attack Messina from the north. His forces used a series of outflanking maneuvers and made very good progress. The Germans realized that they were not strong enough to repulse the powerful Allied forces, and so evacuated their troops from Sicily just as American and British troops arrived in Messina on August 17, 1943. The Allies now had the stepping stone they so desperately needed to launch their invasion of the Italian mainland.

Sicilian farmer gives direction to US infantryman.

German paratroop units in Sicily.

Date:.........................July 9–10, 1943
Participants: ....Sir Harold R. L. G. Alexander, Allied ground commander
                         Montgomery's British forces landed on the southeast coast
                         Patton's Seventh Army landed on the southwest coast
Location of event:......Sicily
Outcome: ....The Axis troops were forced to evacuate the island, and
                         the Allies had a launch pad for the invasion of the Italian
                         mainland

Allies use 4.2 inch mortar Vietra.

JULY 25–OCTOBER 13, 1943

When the Allies successfully landed on the island of Sicily in July 1943, it was clear to the Italian High Command that there was little hope of being able to stop an invasion of the mainland itself. The government collapsed into heated arguments over how matters should be conducted. On July 16 1943, Churchill and Roosevelt exploited the confusion by calling for the Italian people to "Live for civilization," and for them to throw off the yoke of Hitler's rule. Three days later, on July 19, Mussolini met with Hitler in Northern Italy to discuss the situation, and while the meeting was underway, American warplanes bombed Rome and killed around 2,000 people. This stirred up enough ill feeling for King Victor Emmanuel to act, and on July 25 he had Mussolini arrested. The king then replaced him with the Army Chief of Staff, Marshal Pietro Badoglio.

Marshal Badoglio then tried to broker a peace deal with the Allies. However, Hitler moved first and sent additional troops into Italy to disarm the Italian Army. This was a disaster for the Allies, and instead of having an easy time of occupying an undefended Italian peninsula, they had to fight fierce battles with determined German forces. The Italian government continued to discuss the peace deal, and in early September Lieutenant General Maxwell D. Taylor, of the 82nd Airborne Artillery, was secretly parachuted into Rome to negotiate with the Italian government. Although he was pursued by Gestapo agents, an armistice was agreed and a few days later announced to the world on September 8.

The Germans occupied Rome on September 10 and Marshal Badoglio, together with King Victor Emmanuel, fled to an Allied-controlled area in southern Italy. They then established a government-in-exile, and declared war on Germany on October 13, 1943. The Italian forces that were able to do so then switched sides and joined the Allies in attacking German interests.

US Army Air Force Spitfire after forced landing on beach at Salerno.

Warship USS Savanaji, struck by bomb off the coast of Italy.

Dates:	July 25–26, 1943—Mussolini arrested and the Italian Fascist government falls
	Marshal Pietro Badoglio takes over and negotiates with Allies
	September 8, 1943—Italian surrender is announced
	October 13, 1943—Italy declares war on Germany
Participants:	Marshal Pietro Badoglio, Benito Mussolini, King Victor Emmanuel
	Lieutenant General Maxwell D. Taylor
Location of event:	Italy
Outcome:	Italian forces switched sides and declared war on Germany—this gave Hitler another front to defend, putting yet more pressure on men and equipment

Landings at Salerno, Italy.

While the Italians were attempting to broker a peace deal with the Allies following the fall of Sicily in August 1943, the Allies continued to make preparations for a landing on the mainland. On September 3, XIII Corps of Montgomery's Eighth Army was shipped across the Straits of Messina and, after a massive artillery bombardment, landed relatively unopposed at Taranto. This was followed up on September 9—the day after the Italians announced their surrender to the world—by the Americans. The U.S. Fifth Army, under the command of Lieutenant General Mark W. Clark, landed on the coast near Salerno, but the Germans quickly struck back with sustained attacks from their armored units. For some time the battle hung in the balance, and instead of an immediate breakout for Naples, which was 50 miles away, the Americans decided to just hold on to the beachhead and consolidate their positions.

In the end, the combined might of Allied naval guns and aerial bombardment proved too much for German armor, and the Allies were able to move forward again. A week later the American and British forces joined up, and then pushed on toward Naples. With frequent delays due to mined roads and sabotaged bridges, it took them a further two weeks to reach the city, which finally fell on September 30. From then on, however, the brilliant German commander Field Marshal Albert Kesselring exploited the mountainous terrain to hold up the Allied progress. The sticking point was the barrier of fortified positions along a line either side of Monte Casino, where the Germans managed to hold on for six months.

Although the Italian campaign was not the major success for the Allies that it was intended to be—the primary objective being to drive up the

US Troops landing at Naples, Italy.

peninsula into Austria—it did play an important part in the eventual Allied victory. The main reason for this was that the Germans had to pour massive amounts of troops and equipment into defending Italy at a time when these were badly needed elsewhere. With so many fronts to defend, the German military machine was slowly ground away until it had precious little left to make the last stand for the homeland

Dates: ....September 9, 1943
Participants: ....Vth and XIIIth Corps of Montgomery's Eighth Army
U.S. Fifth Army, under Lt Gen Mark W. Clark
2,590 U.S. and British warships. The main group under Vice Admiral Sir A. U. Willis of Force H included: battleships HMSs Nelson, Rodney, Warspite, and Valiant as well as the fleet carriers HMSs Formidable, Indomitable and 7 RN submarines
German forces under Field Marshal Albert Kesselring
Location of event:......Salerno and Taranto, Italy
Outcome: ....The fall of Naples to Allied troops and a determined defense by the Germans of the Viktor Line north of Naples and the Gothic Line above Florence

Hitler and Mussolini in a car.

SEPTEMBER 12–23, 1943

When Mussolini was arrested on July 25, 1943, and his government overthrown, Hitler was furious. He ordered SS-Sturmbannführer Otto Skorzeny to organize and mount a rescue mission. Skorzeny was the most famous and colorful Waffen SS commander of the war, and one of Hitler's favorites. The Allies later gave him the title of "The Most Dangerous Man in Europe." Before he was able to plan the mission, however, German intelligence had to find out where Mussolini was being held. After many weeks they finally worked out where he was being kept captive—this turned out to be a mountain-top resort called the Hotel Campo, which was situated high in the Gran Sasso mountains, in the Apennine range.

Skorzeny quickly swung into action, and assembled a crack team of paratroopers. They made their way through the skies above Italy and staged a daring raid by crash-landing their gliders onto the rocky slopes of the very mountain where Mussolini was being kept prisoner. They rushed the guards and captured the hotel without any resistance. Their prize was quickly evacuated by aircraft and flown to Vienna, where there was a hero's welcome awaiting them on their arrival at the Hotel Continental. Hitler was not there personally, but quickly telephoned to congratulate them on a mission well done.

Hitler then organized a puppet government in German-held northern Italy, with Mussolini at its head; this was known as the Italian Social Republic. For his part in the rescue, Skorzeny was awarded the Knight's Cross and received further promotion. The Nazi-backed government lasted for the rest of the war, and when the Germans in northern Italy surrendered in April 1945, Mussolini was rearrested. This time, Italian Communist partisans wanted to ensure there was no chance of another

Mussolini in uniform.

comeback, and they seized him from the small jail where he was being held at Giulino di Messegra, and he and his mistress, Clara Petacci, were shot and their corpses beaten and publicly displayed, hanging upside-down.

Dates: ....September 12, 1943—Germans rescue Mussolini
September 23, 1943—Mussolini re-establishes a Fascist government
Participants: ....SS-Sturmbannführer Otto Skorzeny, Benito Mussolini
Location of event:......Hotel Campo, in the Appenine mountain range
Outcome: ....The brief establishment of a puppet government in German-held northern Italy; the deaths of Mussolini and his mistress

The Americans' campaign to take the Solomon Islands from the Japanese was a long and militarily expensive affair. By the end of 1943, however, American troops finally reached their main goal—the island of Bougainville. It was hoped to establish airbases there, from which they intended to cut off Rabaul. This was Japan's main forward air and naval base, which was located on the island of New Britain. Denying the Japanese the chance to supply their base was the main objective of the entire Allied offensive in the region. Since Rabaul acted as the center of Japanese air forces in the south Pacific, it was a vital component in their war machine.

On August 15, 1943, a lightning raid was launched from the Russell Islands on Bougainville by eight Corsair fighter aircraft from the Marine Fighter Squadron 214. This was the first Allied attack on the island, and it was mounted in support of American amphibious landings on the island of Vella Lavella. The raid took the Japanese completely by surprise. The Corsairs managed to strafe the Kahili airfield, and in doing so destroyed many aircraft together with much of the base's refuelling equipment.

In the lead up to the arrival of the main Allied invasion force on November 1, 1943, several diversionary attacks were made on nearby islands to create confusion. The Americans landed a total of 14,321 troops from 12 transport ships—these were supported by a minesweeper group. The troops received a rough reception from the entrenched Japanese forces, many of whom were in deep, concealed bunkers. The Japanese sent aircraft from Rabaul to attack the troops as they tried to land, but a determined defense by Allied fighters managed to drive them away before they could do any damage. By nightfall all the troops were ashore, along with 6,200 tons of fuel, rations, and ammunition. The Japanese then sent a large naval force of 19 ships to reinforce Rabaul, but on November 5 this was hit by an Allied air assault, and seven Japanese cruisers were heavily damaged along with two destroyers. By the time this action was over, the Americans had managed to land nearly 34,000 troops and over 23,000 tons of cargo on Bougainville. After much fierce fighting, the majority of the island was taken, although pockets of resistance would hold out until July 1945.

U.S. troops go over the side of a Coast Guard manned combat transport to enter the landing barges at Empress Augusta Bay, Bougainville, as the invasion gets under way.

Date:.........................November 1, 1943
Participants: ....Marine Fighter Squadron 214 and other aircraft from the U.S. Navy, Marine Corps, Army, and Royal New Zealand Air Force.
2nd Marine Parachute Battalion
New Zealand 8th Brigade
U.S. Naval Construction Battalions
Admiral William F. Halsey, U.S. Navy Commander South Pacific
U.S. Naval Task Force 38 under Rear Admiral F.C. Sherman and Task Force 39 under Rear Admiral A.S. Merrill
14,321 invasion troops including the U.S. 3rd Marine Division
Location of event:......Bougainville, Solomon Islands
Outcome: ....The establishment of air bases from which the Allies were able to cut off Japan's main forward air and naval bases at Rabaul

65th Infantry assault wave attacking Butaritari, Yellow Beach Two, find it slow going in the coral bottomed waters. Jap machine gun fire from the right flank makes it more difficult for them. Dargis, Makin Atoll, Gilbert Islands.

NOVEMBER 20, 1943

Toward the end of 1943, war in the Pacific progressed with the Allies continuing to move through the central Pacific, gradually forcing the Japanese back from island to island. Having successfully established themselves on Bougainville in November 1943, the Allies' next targets were the Tarawa and Makin Atolls, in the Gilbert Islands. These small islands were a vital step in the logistics chain up through the Pacific, as their Japanese-constructed airstrips would allow land-based combat, supply and reconnaissance aircraft to operate over much greater ranges. Foremost in the minds of Allied planners was the goal of taking the Marshall Islands, which were of major strategic importance.

The offensive against the Gilbert Islands was code-named Operation "Galvanic," and the U.S. V Amphibious Corps was chosen to make the landings. This was made up of the 2nd Marine Division and the Army's 27th Infantry Division. The Marines were tasked with making the assault on Tarawa Atoll and the Army with taking Makin Atoll, 100 miles north of Tarawa on the route to the Marshalls.

The island of Betio, which was the largest in the Tarawa Atoll, was where the airfield was situated, and as a result was the main focus of the assault. Although it was only a very small island, being just 3 miles long and 600 yards wide, it was extremely heavily fortified. After a brief naval bombardment the troops went ashore in several waves. A lucky few managed to escape serious fire; others, though, sustained very heavy casualties. Reports in the domestic press shocked the American people, with 1,027 killed, 88 missing and 2,292 wounded.

The battle for Tarawa was important in many ways. Not only did it secure the strategically important airbase but it taught the military

Injured marine recieves treatment on the beach at Tarawa.

planners many important lessons. It demonstrated that amphibious assault was the best way to defeat the Japanese, but that for this to work preliminary bombardments had to be heavier and communications had to be improved. These factors received a lot more attention in the months to come, and they certainly contributed to the effectiveness of future assaults.

Date:	November 20, 1943
Participants:	Vth Amphibious Corps
	U.S. 27th Infantry Division
Location of event:	Tarawa and Makin atolls
Outcome:	The capture of the island's airstrips provided strategically important staging posts; the military planners learned valuable lessons for future assaults

Soviet infantry and T-34 tanks move on the offensive.

DECEMBER 24–26, 1943

When Hitler decided to pull his armies back to the line of the Dnepr River after the abortive offensive at Kursk in July 1943, the Soviets wasted little time in mounting a counter-offensive. The German industrial centers had been bombed remorselessly by the Allies, and supplies of raw materials for the war effort were running very short. Consequently, the military could not replace equipment that it lost in the battlefield, whereas in stark contrast the Soviets were producing massive amounts of hardware and training ever-increasing numbers of new troops. On top of this, they received huge quantities of military equipment from the Allies.

The Soviets' new found strength meant that the Red Army could choose exactly where it would strike back at the Wehrmacht, and its commanders decided to make retaking the Ukraine the main priority. This was because the area was rich in natural resources, especially agricultural produce and mineral ores, including iron and manganese. It was felt that if the enemy could be pushed out of the area it would not only deprive Germany of a vital source of supplies, but these same materials could be used to feed the Soviet war machine. A further bonus

was that the Ukraine was close enough to the Romanian oilfields to facilitate a future offensive in that direction.

When the Red Army had assembled sufficient forces, it struck at the weak German defenses and quickly over-ran them. Field Marshal von Manstein—Hitler's Army commander in the Ukraine—was a brilliant tactician, and repeatedly out-maneuvered the Soviet troops. The losses were heavy on both sides; however, unlike their opponents, the Germans were unable to replace more than a fraction of the equipment they lost on the battlefield. When the Soviets launched a massive attack in late January 1944, von Manstein had to pull his troops back and before long the Soviets had liberated the entire Ukraine.

Date:..........................December 24–26, 1943
Participants: ....The Germans:Army Group South under Field Marshal Eric von Manstein
The Soviets:Marshal Ivan S. Konev, commander of the Second Ukrainian Front had seven armies including the Thirty-seventh Army, Seventh Guards Army, Fifty-seventh Army, and the Fifth Guards Tank Army
Location of event:......The Ukraine
Outcome: ....The Germans lost a massive amount of equipment that they were unable to replace, this meant that they had to fall back from the Ukraine

British soldiers shielding themselves in a trench from German bombardment around Anzio.

JANUARY 22–FEBRUARY 16, 1944

When the Allies became bogged down at the German defensive Gustav Line in Italy in late October 1943, whilst trying to fight their way up the Italian peninsula, Allied commanders discussed various methods of bypassing the troublesome defenses. The favorite option was to mount an amphibious landing further north, and as the idea gained credence, it was code-named Operation "Shingle." The plan was dropped for some time, but Churchill, convinced that a quick liberation of Rome was vital, managed to persuade British chiefs of staff that it should be resurrected. The problem was that all the landing craft that could be found were needed for the forthcoming D-Day operation in Normandy. In the end, Churchill won through, and removal of the landing craft for D-Day was delayed for a month.

Anzio was selected as the best site for the landings as it was close to Rome and well within range of Allied aircraft based at Naples. General Mark Clark chose Major General John P. Lucas, who was commander of the U.S. Fifth Army's VI Corps, to head the assault. Lucas was told to try to divert enemy forces away from the Gustav Line to help the Allied units there break through. He was also told to prepare defensive positions to fight off the expected German counter-attack.

General Clark decided to land the largest force that the amount of amphibious shipping would allow, and a massive contingent of troops was assembled. To support the landings, all available Allied aircraft were also thrown into the offensive. This amounted to around 2,600 aircraft, some of which were to attack enemy airfields to reduce the Luftwaffe's ability to strike back. The navy was involved too, with a large flotilla made up of vessels from six countries. The landings went ahead on January 22, 1944 at 2.00am, and achieved complete surprise. By midnight on the same day, over 36,000 men and 3,200 vehicles had been put ashore, with a cost of only 13 men killed

Unfortunately, the orders General Clark had given to Lucas were vague, and Lucas failed to capitalize on the success of the operation. The Germans, who were unable to mount an immediate counter, were amazed that the Allies did not push straight into Rome. They soon mobilized enough troops to strike back, however, with Kesselring moving units from near Rome, and Hitler providing more from Yugoslavia, France and Germany.

The Allies realized that heavy German forces were being built up, and quickly sent more troops to the area—this raised the total of Allied troops to around 100,000. When the German counter-attack came, it was fierce, and far stronger than the Allies had been expecting.

The Anzio offensive was a failure in that it did not provide a quick route around the Gustav Line as intended and it was not until May 1944 that the Allies finally managed to break through. Their troops entered Rome on June 4, 1944, two days before the D-Day invasion.

Dates: .... January 22, 1944—Allies land at Anzio
February 16, 1944—Germans counter-attack against the Anzio beachhead

Participants: .... Maj Gen John P. Lucas, commanded the amphibious assault consisting of: U.S. 3rd Infantry Division; British 1st Infantry Division and 46th Royal Tank Regiment; U.S. 751st Tank Battalion, 504th Parachute Infantry Regiment of U.S. 82nd Airborne Division, and 509th Parachute Infantry Battalion; two British Commando battalions and three battalions of U.S. Army Rangers. The U.S. 45th Infantry Division and Combat Command A (CCA), part of the U.S. 1st Armored Division. The XIIth Tactical Air Command, British Desert Air Force, Coastal Air Force, and the Tactical Bomber Force German forces included: 4th Parachute and Hermann Göring Divisions; the 3rd Panzer Grenadier and 71st Infantry Divisions

Location of event: ...... Anzio and the Gustav Line

Outcome: .... Lucas failed to create an alternative route around the Gustav Line

Russian rockets firing on German positions around Leningrad.

JANUARY 27, 1944

Leningrad, which sits on the shores of Lake Ladoga, was the second largest city in the Soviet Union with a population of three million when the war began. When the German armies invaded the Soviet Union in June 1941, it was one of their prime targets. This was for two reasons—first, as the second biggest city it had great political and psychological significance. Second, its position gave it strategic importance since it blocked the western route around Moscow.

The population of Leningrad responded to calls to defend the city, and more or less every able-bodied individual helped to dig an enormous system of antitank ditches and other defenses. When the Germans arrived on September 8, 1941, they soon found that the city was not going to fall as easily as they had hoped. Instead of wasting valuable armored units of the Army Group North on a pointless assault, the tanks were sent elsewhere, and a long siege began. Hitler knew that the city had a large civilian population, which he did not want to have to feed when his troops finally broke through its defenses. On September 29, 1941, he therefore ordered his commanders to reduce the city to rubble, and a bombardment from land and air began that lasted 872 days.

A certain amount of supplies were brought in by boat across Lake Ladoga, and many of the sick and wounded were evacuated in the same way. Even so, starvation killed in the order of 650,000 people in 1942 alone. When the lake turned to ice in winter, trucks were used to transport large quantities of food and military supplies. In January 1943, a Soviet offensive managed to re-establish the railway link with Moscow, and matters improved for the city's population. A year later, in January 1944, another major Soviet offensive drove off the remaining German troops, and the 900-day siege was over. Estimates suggest that over a million Soviets were killed during this time and Leningrad remains a symbol of Nazi brutality.

Russian T-34 tanks advancing.

Date:........................January 27, 1944
Participants: ....The Red Army under Marshal Zhukov
                    The German Army Group North
Location of event:......Leningrad
Outcome: ....Estimates suggest that over a million Soviets were killed

Back to a Coast Guard assault transport comes this Marine after two days and nights of Hell on the beach of Eniwetok in the Marshall Islands. His face is grimey with coral dust but the light of battle stays in his eyes.

January 31, 1944

The Marshall Islands were a major goal for the Allies in the Pacific, as their capture would provide a major stepping stone toward both the Carolines and the Marianas. They would provide not only vital airstrips but also new bases for the U.S. Navy. The Marshalls had been held by the Japanese since World War I, and they had used them as reconnaissance, combat and logistics bases for much of their war effort in the central Pacific. The primary Japanese naval base in the Marshalls was on Kwajalein Island, but there were also several other islands of great military importance. Roi-Namur, for instance, was the main Japanese airbase in the area.

The offensive against Roi-Namur was launched on January 31, 1944, but before the Marines went in the island came in for very heavy naval and air bombardment. Around 6,000 tons of high explosives were dropped on the enemy, with the naval fire support vessels moving in very close to shore. In the action the Marines lost 313 killed and 502 wounded, as compared with all but 90 of the estimated 3,563 Japanese garrison force being killed.

Unlike most of the previous assaults, the taking of Kwajalein Island was executed almost perfectly on February 1. This was achieved for two reasons:first, the troops were trained extremely well, and second, the task force commander wanted to make sure that the preliminary bombardment was as effective as it could possibly be. The casualties were light on the American side, with only 173 killed and 793 wounded, whereas the Japanese lost an estimated 4,823 Japanese garrison troops.

When American troops landed on Majuro Atoll on February 1, they found that the Japanese troops had all been evacuated, and so there was

Marine riflemen under fire leap from a just-beached amphibian tractor in the January 1944 landing.

no loss of life. The next target was Eniwetok Atoll, and here the fighting was intense; around 350 American troops were killed, and 860 wounded. The Japanese lost about 3,400 killed and 66 were taken prisoner. Rather than risk further Allied casualties, the four remaining Japanese bases were simply cut off from resupply. It is believed that of the 13,700 soldiers stationed there, 7,440 died from bombing, starvation or disease.

Losing the Marshall Islands to the Allies was a major blow for the Japanese, and it caused them to abandon their air and naval bases at Truk Island in the Carolines, which considerably weakened their ability to operate in the Central Pacific.

Date:.........................January 31, 1944
Participants: .............U.S. Marine Corps 4th Division under Marine Maj Gen Harry Schmidt was landed by the Northern Task Force under Rear Admiral Richard L. Conolly
The U.S. Army's 7th Infantry Division under Army Maj Gen Charles H. Corlett was landed by the Southern Task Force under Rear Admiral Richmond Kelly Turner
Vth Amphibious Corps Reconnaissance Company and the U.S. Army's 2nd Battalion, 106th Infantry Regiment, 27th Division under Army Lt Col Frederick B. Sheldon were landed by the Majuro Attack Force under Rear Admiral Harry W. Hill
Location of event:......Marshall Islands
Outcome: ....The Japanese abandoned their large air and naval bases at Truk Island

Last ship from the Crimea.

APRIL 8–MAY 9, 1944

After pushing the Germans back across the Dnepr River in the Ukraine in January 1944, the Soviets consolidated their territorial gains and prepared for the next offensive. At this late stage in the war their greatest military asset was the amount of equipment and the numbers of troops they had. In order to exploit this they steered away from localized encirclement operations and instead chose to move forward on broad fronts. The philosophy behind this was that the Germans could respond to concentrated actions with the limited equipment they had left, whereas they simply could not cope with large-scale maneuvers. This strategy was helped considerably by Hitler's blind refusal to allow his troops to fall back when necessary, and as a result the Soviets inexorably ground down the German military machine.

Having defeated German armies in the Ukraine (although fighting there would continue into the summer), the next target was the Crimea and especially the liberation of Sevastopol, with its vital Black Sea port. In November 1943 the Red Army (in the form of the 4th Ukrainian Front under Marshal Fyodor I. Tolbukhin) pushed forward along the Sea of Azov, in the process cutting off the German and Romanian troops in the Crimea. He then joined forces with Marshal Andrei I. Yeremenko's Coastal Army and broke into the Crimea. Huge artillery bombardments of Sevastopol had their desired effect: in spite of Hitler's insistence on no surrender, Sevastopol was liberated on May 12, 1944—the Germans attempted to withdraw their garrison by sea, but only managed to extricate half of their 65,000 troops. The rest were left behind to face the Red Army.

Soviet tanks supported by a Maxim M1910 machine gun crew.

Dates: ....April 8, 1944—Soviet troops break through into Crimea
May 12, 1944—Soviet troops recapture Sevastopol.
Participants: ....German Seventeenth Army
Soviet 4th Ukrainian Front (Tolbukhin) and Coastal Army
(Yeremenko)
Location of event:......The Crimea and Sevastopol
Outcome: ....The Soviets regained their major port on the Black Sea;
the Germans lost vast numbers of men and equipment - a
military disaster from which they never recovered

Allied troops land in Normandy, France during Operation "Overlord".

By 1944, the Americans had shipped enough men and equipment across the Atlantic for a fresh Allied offensive in western Europe aimed directly at Germany to be possible. An enormous force was assembled under Supreme Allied Commander, Dwight D. Eisenhower, including 3,000 landing craft, 2,500 other ships, and 500 naval escort and bombardment ships. After a series of delays due to bad weather and equipment supply problems, the invasion force landed on the Normandy coast on June 6, 1944. The crossing was supported by 13,000 aircraft, which held the air space and also mounted continuous attacks on German defenses and inland communications systems.

The invasion was code-named Operation "Overlord," and since the Germans were expecting the attack to come at Calais, it was relatively unopposed. Nearly a million men were put ashore in the first 10 days—this was helped by the French resistance who cut telephone lines and blew up bridges to slow down the German military response. Many troops were airlifted across the Channel in preliminary assaults to take key objectives in advance of the main landings: they either landed by parachute or glider. These elite soldiers suffered especially high casualties; however, they succeeded in taking and holding their objectives.

In the lead up to Operation "Overlord" a massive campaign of disinformation was mounted in order to confuse the German High Command as to where the invasion would land. This was particularly successful, a good example being that a powerful force of SS Panzers was lured into going to the south of France in the mistaken belief that the Allies were intending to land there. Once they realized that the invasion was actually taking place in Normandy, they attempted to make their way north. However, French resistance fighters and Allied aircraft had

Landing on the coast of France under heavy Nazi machine gun fire are these American soldiers, shown just as they left the ramp of a Coast Guard landing boat.

blown up the railways, so they had to go by road. On their way the resistance blew up so many bridges and felled so many trees in their path that progress was slowed to a crawl, and by the time they reached the north they were too late to influence the landings.

Date:..........................June 6, 1944
Participants: ....3,500 amphibious craft, 2,500 other ships, and 500 naval vessels; 13,000 aircraft150,000 vehicles and 850,000 men including:
The British Second Army, under General Miles C. Dempsey
British 6th Airborne Division
British 3rd Infantry Division
Canadian 3rd Division
U.S. First Army, under General Omar N. Bradley
U.S. 82nd and 101st Airborne Divisions
U.S. 1st, 4th, and 29th Divisions
U.S. Vth and VIIth Corps
German Army Group B, commanded by Field Marshal Erwin Rommel
German Seventh Army, commanded by General Friedrich Dollmann
German 352nd Coast Division
German 21st Panzer Division
German 6th Parachute Regiment
Location of event:......The Normandy coast of France
Outcome: ....The Allies successfully launched their invasion of Western Europe, landing over 850,000 men and 150,000 vehicles in three weeks

German V1 flying bomb production line.

June 13, 1944

On June 13, 1944 the inhabitants of London discovered to their horror that the Nazis had successfully developed a new terror weapon, known to the Germans as the Fieseler Fi-103 V1 flying bomb, or V1 for short. The "V" stood for Vergeltungswaffe or "vengeance weapon"—the hapless civilians who had to endure its regular flights, however, nicknamed it the "Buzz Bomb" or "Doodlebug," after the strange sound it made. This noise was generated by the flying bomb's Argus pulse-jet engine, and since it flew at low altitudes—only 2,000-3000 feet—the sound could be heard for miles. The real threat, however, came when the motor cut out, for then the 25-foot-long bomb would come plummeting to earth, killing or maiming anyone within range.

The V1 was developed on a top-secret development site at Peenemünde, on a peninsula that stretched out into the Baltic Sea. It was deliberately located in an isolated and secluded position so that few would know of its existence. An entire sealed community was constructed there, and staff moved their entire families into the site's housing facilities. Only a few personnel were allowed to leave the area—this way maximum security was established.

The bomb itself had an operating range of around 160 miles, and flew at speeds of between 360 and 400mph. It had an average flight time of 22 minutes and carried a 1,870lb warhead. It could be launched either from a huge catapult or from beneath a large aircraft. In order to get the maximum range and accuracy from the V1s, some were carried to altitude and then released by modified twin-engined Heinkel He111 bombers.

Between June 1944 and March 29, 1945, the Nazis launched 9,251 V1 flying bombs against England. However, only 2,419 reached their targets. The RAF managed to down over 2,000 V1s, antiaircraft fire shot down 1,971, and barrage balloons accounted for a further 278. They killed around 5,500 people and injured about another 16,000.

Date:.......................June 13, 1944
Participants: ....The Fieseler Fi-103 V1 flying bomb
Location of event:......London
Outcome: ....5,500 people killed and 16,000 injured

B-29 "Super Fortress" in flight.

With the introduction of the Boeing B-29 Superfortress, the Americans had their first long-range bomber. As soon as it was in service, plans were made to use this new capability to bomb Japan itself, primarily with the intention of disabling the country's war industries. The bases captured on the islands in the Central Pacific were still too far away to stage a bombing raid on Japan, and so the decision was taken to take off from China. The Chengtu area was closest to Japan, but as there were no suitably located airstrips in the region it was necessary to specially construct them using local manual labor. All the necessary supplies—fuel, ammunition and bombs had to be specially flown in for the mission over the Himalayas.

The target the planners chose was the Imperial Iron and Steel Works at Yawata, which was located on the island of Kyushu. The raid was scheduled for June 15, 1944, and it was intended that 75 B-29s take part. On the day, however, one aircraft crashed on take-off, and several others had technical faults causing them to turn back. Sixty-four aircraft made their way toward their target. The lead aircraft was called the "Postville Express," and was piloted by Major Humphrey, and it also carried the strike commander, Brigadier General Laverne G. Saunders. Spread across the other aircraft were 11 American war correspondents and photographers—it was intended that the first major raid on Japanese industry was going to be big news back home.

The raid was not a great success in itself—seven aircraft were lost and little damage was done to the target. It did, however, distract the Japanese from the Allied attack on Saipan the same day, from where future B-29 raids against the Japanese mainland would be conducted.

Aerial photograph of Yawata during the American bombardment.

B-29 refuelling.

Date:.........................June 15, 1944
Participants: ....64 B-29 aircraft led by Major Humphrey in the "Postville Express"
Location of event:......The Imperial Iron and Steel Works at Yawata, on the island of Kyushu
Outcome: ....The raid distracted the Japanese from the Allied attack on Saipan

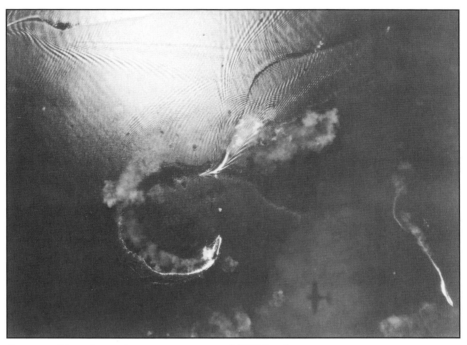

Japanese ships take evasive manoeuvres to avoid US bombers.

JUNE 15–JULY 9, 1944

As Allied forces made their way toward the Japanese homelands, the Japanese defending the many islands in the region became increasingly desperate. By June 1944, the next target for the Allies was Saipan—this was part of the Marianas Archipelago, and therefore in Japanese territory. Prime Minister Hideki Tojo optimistically believed that the defensive perimeter around the Japanese Home Islands, which included Saipan, was strong enough to fight off Allied invasion forces.

To ensure that the civilian populations would do as they were told, the Japanese military put out propaganda saying that the American troops would commit atrocities on them if they allowed themselves to be taken. Vice Admiral Chuichi Nagumo—who had been in charge of the attack on Pearl Harbor—was put in command of the 30,000 soldiers on Saipan. The Japanese philosophy was simple—to fight the American forces as soon as they tried to set foot on the shore. Consequently, when the U.S. Marines began their assault on June 15, 1944, they came under intense fire. The Marines took extremely heavy losses, with 2,000 casualties on the first day alone. They did, however, manage to land 20,000 troops successfully by nightfall.

It took five days of continuous fighting to suppress the defenders, and apart from a number of Japanese troops holed up in a group of caves the island was considered secure by June 20. The Americans had not realized how many Japanese soldiers were still alive, however, and during the night of July 7, the remaining 3,000 troops rushed the Americans in the largest suicide charge of the war. This took them by surprise, but after a night of heavy fighting, the Japanese were completely annihilated.

A Grumman F6F warms up on the deck of the USS Lexington in preparation for a strike on Saipan.

Of the 30,000 Japanese defenders, only 1,000 survived—many of these being too badly injured to kill themselves. A total of 22,000 civilians also perished in the assault, a large number of whom were pushed or jumped over cliffs. The American casualty count was 16,525. The fall of Saipan was a great shock to Prime Minister Tojo, and his government fell shortly afterward in July 1944. Hopes for a negotiated armistice were dashed, and it was clear to many in Japan that the war was lost.

Date: ....June 15–July 9, 1944
Participants: ....The Japanese forces consisted of 30,000 troops under the command of Lt Gen Yoshitsugu Saito and Vice Admiral Chiuchi Nagumo
Vth Amphibious Corps totaling 71,034 Marine and Army troops
U.S. 2nd Marine Division under Maj Gen Thomas E. Watson
U.S. 4th Marine Division under Maj Gen Harry Schmidt
U.S. 27th Infantry Division under Maj Gen Ralph C. Smith
Location of event: ......Saipan, Marianas Archipelago
Outcome: ....The fall of the Japanese government

JULY 20, 1944

On the morning of July 20, 1944 many of Hitler's highest-ranking officers mounted an attempt to kill him. One of them, General Claus Schenk von Stauffenberg, had placed a briefcase packed with British-made explosives near Hitler during a meeting with senior members of the General Staff at his headquarters in Rastenburg, East Prussia. This HQ was also known as the "wolf's lair," and was Hitler's command post for the eastern front.

The assassination attempt was the first stage in a planned coup, which became known as the July plot. This was led by many senior army staff officers, including Field Marshal Erwin von Witzleben and General Ludwig von Beck. The bomb went off at 12:42 local time, and General von Stauffenberg, who had left the room, heard the explosion and assumed that Hitler was dead.

The bomb had failed to kill the Führer—he escaped with minor burns, concussion and impaired hearing; three other people in the room, however, were killed. The German news agencies were quick to reassure the populace, telling them that Hitler was slightly injured but that he had still managed to keep his appointment with the Italian leader Benito Mussolini. The agencies also said that the German people were deeply grateful that no serious harm had come to their leader and that fate had allowed him to "accomplish his great task."

Hitler with Keitel and Göring to his right and Bormann to his left after the July 20, 1944, bomb plot. Hitler is holding his right arm, slightly injured in the blast.

Von Stauffenberg was arrested later the same day and shot. The other main conspirators were also rounded up, eight of whom were hanged with piano wire from meat-hooks. Their executions were filmed and shown to Hitler, who then ordered senior members of the Nazi Party and the armed forces to watch it as well. Field Marshal Erwin Rommel, who was implicated in the plot, was offered the chance to commit suicide, which he took. A purge was then mounted by Hitler's security services, and thousands of the plotters' family members were also forced to commit suicide or sent to concentration camps. In all, somewhere in the order of 20,000 people were killed as a result of Hitler's lust for revenge. This was intended as a clear warning to anyone who might have contemplated mounting another attempt on the Führer's life.

Date: .... July 20, 1944
Participants: .... General Stauffenberg, Field Marshal Erwin von Witzleben, General Ludwig von Beck, General Erwin Rommel
Location of event: ...... Hitler's headquarters in Rastenberg, East Prussia.
Outcome: .... 20,000 people—families, friends, and associates of the plotters were killed or sent to concentration camps by Hitler; he mistrusted the army even more.

First flag on Guam on boat hook mast. Two U.S. officers plant the American flag on Guam eight minutes after U.S. Marines and Army assault troops landed on the Central Pacific island on July 20, 1944.

JULY 21–AUGUST 10, 1944

After Allied forces captured Saipan in July 1944, the next major island in the Marianas Archipelago chain was Guam. This is the largest island in the region, measuring 212 square miles (549sq km) in total. In the north there is a limestone plateau, and in the south a ridge of volcanic hills. When the Japanese invaded Guam in 1941, it was under U.S. Navy administration—as it had been since 1899. The 400-man American garrison was easily overwhelmed by the 5,000 Japanese troops who took part in the assault. When the Americans returned on July 21, 1944, however, matters had changed considerably, and a massive invasion force began their offensive. Although the Japanese put up intense fire, the combined Army and Marine troops made their way ashore and established themselves.

Gradually, the Japanese were flushed out of their defensive positions, often heavily constructed concrete bunkers, and the island fell to the Americans. On the night of July 25-26, the Japanese, as on previous occasions, staged a massed suicide charge, similar to that on Saipan. This time, however, there were 5,000 men involved. Over 2,500 of them died in the attempt, and while these charges were feared by the Americans, it was better than trying to extract the enemy from deep bunkers. Many Japanese troops fled into the jungle, from where they continued to harass the Americans. The American casualty figures in taking Guam were 1,000 killed and 7,000 wounded. The Japanese lost around 10,000 killed.

The crew of the USS South Dakota stands with bowed heads, while Chaplain N. D. Lindner reads the benediction held in honor of fellow shipmates killed in the air action off Guam on June 19, 1944.

After the major hostilities had been completed, American construction battalions started building airfields and associated facilities to prepare for the next stage in the war. Once completed, the bases were made ready for the large numbers of B-29 bombers and other aircraft which were needed to bomb Japan's industrial centers and to help in the invasion of the remaining islands.

Date:........................July 21–August 10, 1944
Participants: ............U.S. IIIrd Amphibious Corps
　　　　　　　　　　　Japanese occupation forces
Location of event:......Guam, Marianas Archipelago
Outcome: ....The construction of a strategically significant airfield which provided a vital forward supply base for further Allied operations

A Water Buffalo, loaded with Marines, churns through the sea bound for beaches of Tinian Island near Guam.

JULY 24–AUGUST 1, 1944

With the fall of Saipan and Guam, the last remaining island in the Marianas Archipelago of military significance was Tinian. This is situated 80 miles north of Guam, and a few miles south of Saipan, from where the actual invasion was launched. Tinian had been designated by Allied war planners to be the site of a major airbase once it had been captured. It already had three airfields and the Japanese were busy building a fourth. The island was ideally located for long-range B-29 Superfortress bombers to strike at the Japanese mainland, and so was an important invasion target.

The American assault on Tinian began on July 24, 1944, where there were 9,162 Japanese army and navy troops ready to fight them off. The offensive began previously with a 13-day naval bombardment, and included the use of napalm bombs—it was the first time this incendiary weapon had ever been used in warfare. After the artillery barrages ceased the invasion began, although the first apparent landings were a feint. The 2nd Marine Division managed to make it look as though it was about to attack on the southern coast, and this drew Japanese forces into defensive positions there. Meanwhile, the 4th Marine Division attacked from the north and successfully landed a large contingent of troops. After many days of fierce fighting, the Americans finally defeated the Japanese defenders on August 1, 1944.

The improvements in command, control and training meant that the operation was carried out with unusual precision, and it is considered by many to have been the best-executed amphibious action of the war. The Americans lost 328 dead and 1,571 wounded, whereas few of the more than 9,000 Japanese troops survived. Some of these were killed in action, whereas others chose to commit suicide by jumping off cliffs.

Japanese plane shot down as it attempted to attack USS Kitkun Bay. Near Mariana Islands.

Tinian became the site of one of the biggest engineering projects of the entire war, and before long four vast 2,850-yard runways were operational. A total of 19,000 American combat missions were launched against Japan from Tinian.

Date:.........................July 24–August 1, 1944
Participants: ....Task Force Five One, under Rear Admiral Harry W. Hill
U.S. 2nd and 4th Marine Divisions,
under Maj Gen Roy S. Geiger
9,162 Japanese Army and Navy troops
Location of event:......Tinian, Marianas Archipelago
Outcome: ....A total of 19,000 American combat missions were launched against Japan from Tinian, including the aircraft which dropped the atomic bombs on Hiroshima and Nagasaki

JULY 25–30, 1944

Once the troops who crossed the Channel in the D-Day landings of Operation "Overlord" had established a secure bridgehead, further men and supplies poured into Normandy in an unceasing stream. This provided them with enough firepower to organize their break out; the plan was code-named Operation "Cobra," and came from an idea first proposed by the U.S. Third Army's General George Patton. The operation was led by the U.S. First Army under the command of General Omar Bradley. Before the new offensive began, a massive aerial bombardment was staged by more than 3,000 aircraft on July 25, including 1,500 heavy bombers of the U.S. Eighth Army Air Force. Unfortunately, at least 500 Allied troops were killed by American bombers dropping their bombs short of their targets. The carpet bombing raids weakened the German defenses sufficiently for the Allied troops to punch through, and once again headway was made.

Hitler was determined to push the Allies back, and against all the advice of his army commanders ordered his Panzer units to mount a counter-attack. On August 7, 1944, the Germans threw almost every surviving armored unit in the area into the offensive. The U.S. Army had 750 of the latest Sherman tanks and 15 well-equipped divisions as compared with the Germans' 150 tanks and nine battle-weary divisions.

A squadron of bombers from the US Eighth Army Air Force during Operation "Cobra".

After being hit by Allied aircraft, the out-numbered Panzers were unable to hold out, and soon most of the German troops were retreating in disarray.

From this point onward, the Allies fought their way through northern France, surrounding German troops in Brittany, and then moving rapidly around and encircling further units in Normandy from the rear. Operation "Cobra" had been a great success, and it cleared the way for the Allies to push forward toward their goal of invading German soil.

Date:	July 25–30, 1944
Participants:	U.S. 1st Armored Division
	U.S. First and Third Armies
	Fighter-bombers, medium and heavy bombers of the U.S. Eighth Air Force
	British Second Army
	Canadian troops
Location of event:	The Contentin peninsula, Normandy, France
Outcome:	The operation cleared the way for the Allies to push forward towards their goal of invading German soil

Operation Dragoon - Amphibious vehicles on the beach.

AUGUST 15, 1944

Ten weeks after the D-Day offensive was launched, a second Allied invasion took place on the southern coast of Nazi-occupied France between Toulon and Cannes. Its mission was to create a second front to draw German forces away from the Allies' armies fighting to break out of Normandy. The plans were originally code-named Operation "Anvil," but since Churchill felt he had been dragooned by the Americans into accepting the idea, it was re-named Operation "Dragoon."

The offensive was launched from the Mediterranean Sea on August 15, 1944, with 1,000 ships, 3,000 aircraft, and 300,000 troops. Although the area was where Hitler had been expecting the main invasion to occur, the Normandy landings had drawn away the bulk of his troops and armor. This meant that the landings were relatively unopposed and casualties were less than expected.

The bulk of the assault force was made up of American troops—three divisions of infantry, as well as airborne and special service task forces. To provide back-up, they received support from French commandos and British paratroopers. The landings were well co-ordinated, and on the first day over 94,000 troops and 11,000 vehicles were landed. They managed to take 20 miles in the first 24 hours—this success stimulated French resistance fighters in Paris to stage a major uprising. The bulk of the casualties were among the British and American paratroopers, many of whom landed in the sea and drowned. It is thought that around 1,300 Allied soldiers died in the first two days.

The American and French troops managed to capture Toulon and Marseilles within two weeks. The German Nineteenth Army was unable to withstand the onslaught of the massive Allied invasion force, and soon

Operation Dragoon - 1st Abn, 7th US Army with German POW's.

fell back into a rapid retreat northward along the Rhone Valley. By mid-September, Allied troops moving northward linked up near Dijon with others moving south from the Normandy landings. They then combined forces and turned their attention toward the German Siegfried Line.

Date:.........................August 15, 1944
Participants: .............U.S. 3rd Infantry Division at Alpha Beach (Cavalaire-sur-Mer)
U.S. 45th Infantry Division at Delta Beach (Saint-Tropez)
U.S. 36th Infantry Division at Camel Beach (Saint-Raphael).
1st Airborne Task Force
U.S. 1st Special Service Force
British 2nd Independent Parachute Brigade
French commando groups
German Nineteenth Army
Location of event:......The coast of southern France between Toulon and Cannes
Outcome: ....Allied troops moved north and linked up with others moving south from the Normandy landings. They then combined forces and attacked the Siegfried Line.

An American officer and a French partisan crouch behind an auto during a street fight in Paris.

AUGUST 25, 1944

By the time of the D-Day landings, Paris had been occupied by German forces for four years and much of the population was desperate to shake off its oppressors. Others, however, had conspired with the Nazis to persecute the Jews and to round up and send hundreds of thousands of French citizens to Germany to work as slave laborers in the production of war materials. By 1945 the vast majority of the forced labor conscripted from eastern Europe had died from illness, starvation or ill-treatment. The large numbers of French workers therefore formed the bulk of Germany's industrial production force. Most of the collaborators who organized these affairs were members of the Vichy government

The city of Paris itself was ostensibly a place of gaiety, with many theatres and dance halls, and its famous café culture. However, it also had an underlying layer of terror and repression caused by the brutality of the Gestapo and the SS. A thriving resistance movement was established, and although its activities were largely insignificant before the D-Day landings, it did manage to stockpile a large collection of weapons. As times went on, food prices rose, and things got much harder for the average Parisian inhabitant; consequently, more and more people joined the ranks of the resistance.

Once Allied troops had managed to break out from Normandy in August, they defeated the German Seventh Army and fought their way toward Paris. The resistance fighters eagerly awaited the arrival of Allied forces, and when the second series of landings on the south coast of France (Operation "Dragoon") proved successful they could wait no longer and rose up. After some fierce fighting, the German garrison commander General von Choltitz tried to arrange a truce with the Free

US Armored car in Paris.

French under Charles de Gaulle. However, he proved to be impossible to deal with and the talks broke down. Hitler ordered von Choltitz to burn Paris to the ground, but he disobeyed the Führer, and instead surrendered on August 25. As a result of his actions, Paris escaped the destruction that so many other cities experienced and the city was liberated.

Date:........................August 25, 1944
Participants: ....German garrison under General Dietrich von Choltitz
Free French 2nd Armored Division under Jacques-Philippe Leclerc
Location of event:......Paris
Outcome: ....The liberation of Paris

Overturned German tank following Russian attack near Bucharest.

At the beginning of World War II, Romania quickly aligned herself with Germany. This was mainly because of the threat of invasion by the Soviet Union—the Romanians felt that if they aligned themselves with Hitler, Stalin would not dare invade their small country. Consequently, when Germany attacked the Soviet Union in Operation "Barbarossa," Romania took a major part in the invasion.

Romanian authorities were also merciless in the rounding up and killing of thousands of Jews, either by firing squad or through starvation in concentration camps. Territories in the Ukraine were given to Romania for her part in its invasion—these were named "Transnistria," and were ruled by a military administration. Massacres of thousands of Russian Jews continued in these areas throughout the war—the total number is thought to be around 250,000. When the Red Army fought its way down through the Crimea in the spring of 1944, it continued remorselessly toward Romania. The main priority was to take the oilfields—this would not only bolster Soviet supplies but it would fatally wound the German military machine, as there were few other sources available to it.

As the Soviets began a major offensive against Romania on August 20, 1944, the standing government under General Ion Antonescu was overthrown by opposition leaders led by King Mihai. After the war Antonescu was tried and executed. The new government quickly agreed an armistice with the Soviet Union on August 23, 1944, and under Allied surrender terms declared war on Germany. Over one million Romanian soldiers then joined the Soviet troops and fought with them through Hungary and into Germany. The armistice terms also stipulated that Romania would pay war reparations in produce equivalent to $300 million. This included grain, oil, machinery and ships.

General Ion Antonescu decorating his troops.

Date:..........................August 31, 1944
Participants: ....The Red Army
General Ion Antonescu
King Mihai
Location of event:......Bucharest
Outcome: ....Romania surrendered and joined forces with the Soviets.
Germany lost access to vital oilfields and agricultural produce

A Nazi soldier, heavily armed, carries ammunition boxes forward with companion in territory taken by their counter- offensive in this scene from captured German film.

SEPTEMBER 1–13, 1944

In the early part of September 1944, Allied forces were making good progress through France and toward their goal of invading Germany. They liberated many towns and cities, including Verdun, Dieppe, Artois, Rouen, Abbeville, Antwerp and Brussels. In many of these places there were useful ports, and this helped the Allies shorten their supply lines immensely. The local populations were usually so pleased to see the advancing soldiers that large crowds of cheering people would often assemble before the fighting had completely ceased.

Once the defending Wehrmacht forces—including the much vaunted Fifteenth German Army—had given way, the gains made by the advancing Allies were spectacular. There were a few brief hold-ups, including fierce fire-fights at the Ghent and Leopold canals, but against the might of the Allied invasion army, the Germans soon gave way and most of Belgium was liberated in early September. This was seen by many as a sign of the increasing weakness of their enemy.

The ease of progress led to a prevailing mood of reckless optimism, and despite warnings from British code-breaking activities at Bletchley Park, many believed that Germany was already finished. The truth of the matter, however, was that the short stands were simply to give German troops time to cross waterways so that they could withdraw to safety behind the Siegfried Line. This was a system of concrete pillboxes and bunkers that had been built along the western frontier of Germany in the 1930s. In 1944, it established a barrier behind which the retreating German troops could rest, secure in the knowledge that, for a short time at least, they had a safe haven.

American soldiers, stripped of all equipment, lie dead, face down in the slush of a crossroads somewhere on the western front.

Dates:	September 1–4, 1944—Verdun, Dieppe, Artois, Rouen, Abbeville, Antwerp, and Brussels liberated by Allies September 13, 1944—U.S. troops reach the Siegfried Line
Participants:	Fifteenth German Army under General Gustav von Zangen Allied forces:British, American, Canadian, Polish, Dutch Belgian, French, Czechoslovakian, Norwegian, Danish, Luxembourg, as well as the Resistance. These included: The Welsh Guards. 1st Battalion, the Worcestershire Regiment R.E.M.E. and R.A.S.C. Belgian Independent Brigade 1st Battalion, U.S. 66th Armored Regiment U.S. 364th Infantry Regiment Canadian First Army including VIII Recce Regiment (14 CH) 4th Canadian Armored Division
Location of event:	Eastern France and Belgium
Outcome:	The Germans withdraw to safety behind the Siegfried Line, forcing the Allies to build up sufficient forces to break through

General Douglas MacArthur.

SEPTEMBER 15–OCTOBER 13, 1944

The invasion of Peleliu, in the Palau Islands in the Pacific, was deemed necessary by the Americans for several reasons. Although it was only a tiny island, it was a vital link in the communications system the Japanese used to co-ordinate their forces in the Philippines. The large number of enemy troops based there also represented a real threat to Allied forces moving through the area, and so the island could not simply be bypassed.

General Douglas MacArthur's plan called for Peleliu to be taken so that it could be used as a stepping stone in the invasion of the Philippines. The operation was code-named "Stalemate II," and it was set to begin on September 15, 1944. While the planning was underway, the navy mounted a blockade of the island so that it could not be reinforced or resupplied. As with previous amphibious landings, the assault was preceded by a massive naval bombardment. For three days the island's defenses were pounded by naval artillery; however, it was ineffective against the deep concrete bunkers the Japanese had constructed.

Many of these were inter-linked, forming an underground fortification of impressive proportions.

The actual assault was staged on the 15 on the island's west coast by three separate forces of U.S. Marines. The 1st Marine Division attacked the left side, the 5th Marines went for the center, and the 7th Marines attacked to the right. As the troops went in, they took fire from heavily fortified machine gun nests and from well-concealed snipers. The Japanese were determined to prevent a beachhead being established, and they fought furiously. The Marines slowly inched their way inland, gradually taking ground from the enemy. After a week of intense combat, the southern end of the island was secured, including the high ground above the airfield. While the fighting was going on, large quantities of supplies had also been brought ashore.

Although the use of close air support was perfected in the fight for Peleliu, the underground fortresses required a different approach. Since more than 500 caves and bunkers were being occupied by Japanese troops, a good solution was desperately needed. This was provided in the form of long-range flame throwers—these were mounted on amphibious tractors and were extremely effective in dealing with soldiers in underground emplacements.

The casualty figures for the battle of Peleliu were the highest up to that point in the war in the Pacific for a single operation, with 1,336 Marines killed and 5,450 wounded. The U.S. infantry lost over 400 killed and around 3,000 were wounded. It is thought that around 10,695 Japanese troops were killed.

Date:	September 15–October 13, 1944
Participants:	U.S. 1st, 5th and 7th Marines
	U.S. naval blockade force
	Japanese garrison
Location of event:	Peleliu, Palau Islands
Outcome:	The capture of Peleliu was of great strategic importance, for it severed a critical link in the Japanese communications system

Paratroopers from the US 82nd and 101st Airborne divisions landing near Nijmegen.

The thrust toward the north German plain was composed of two operations—"Market," an airborne attack by British 1st Airborne Division, the Polish Parachute Brigade, and paratroops from U.S. 82nd and 101st Airborne Divisions on Nijmegen, Eindoven, and Arnhem to take bridges across the Maas, Waal, and lower Rhine; and "Garden," the ground attack along the cleared route by XXXth Corps of the British Second Army.

The main purpose of the high-speed attack was to give the Allies a chance to cross the Rhine before the Germans could mobilize to stop them. This would also cut off the German forces in western Holland and outflank the well-fortified Siegfried Line. If it were successful, it would leave the Allies positioned to drive across the open plains of northern Germany—an area that would be very hard to defend. It was genuinely believed that the plan could shorten the war by a year.

A force of 10,000 paratroops was assembled, and on the morning of September 17, 1944, the operation began. The U.S. drops worked brilliantly and Nijmegen and Eindhoven were seized, At the same time the ground forces began moving, but the attack stalled almost immediately—a story that would continue as the armored thrust attempted to drive along a narrow axis. The British troops from the 1st Airborne Division that landed near Arnhem were dropped into an area defended by two German divisions—the 9th (Hohenstaufen) and 10th (Frundsberg) SS-Panzer Divisions—and suffered enormous casualties as a

British Paratroopers from the 1st Airborne division landing near Arnhem.

result. They did, however, manage to secure the north side of the bridge they were sent to seize. Although they were meant to hold out for only four days, they did so for nine without relief. In the end, Montgomery ordered them to break out and attempt to join other Allied forces.

Of the 10,000 men who were dropped into Arnhem, only 2,300 managed to get out—1,400 were killed in the action, and over 6,000 were taken prisoner. Operation "Market Garden" was a spectacular failure, and with it ended the chance of an early conclusion to the war.

Date:	September 1944
Participants:	Arnhem—British 1st Airborne Division, Polish Parachute Brigade
	Nijmegen and Eindhoven—U.S. 101st and 82nd Airborne Divisions
	British Second Army
Location of event:	Holland
Outcome:	At Arnhem, 1,400 killed in the action, and over 6,000 taken prisoner. Elsewhere, the advance of Allied forces to the Rhine

Gen. Douglas MacArthur wades ashore during initial landings at Leyte, P.I.

OCTOBER 20–26, 1944

In order for the Allies to attack the mainland of Japan, it was first necessary to rid the Philippines of their Japanese invaders. They had such a large force there that Allied operations would be impossible until they were removed. If the Philippines could be taken, it would cut many of the sea-routes the Japanese used to communicate with her extensive naval bases spread throughout the islands of the East Indies.

Although the island of Luzon was a primary goal, it was so heavily defended that a staging post was needed—at this stage in 1944 American forces were still a long way south of the Philippines. The island of Leyte was chosen as the ideal location, and so a full-scale invasion of this large island was planned. Around 110 miles long and between 10 and 15 miles wide, Leyte has deep water and sandy beaches along its east coast. This was ideal for amphibious assaults and resupply operations. Along the spine of the island is a forested mountain range which reaches to over 4,400 feet. This area is full of caves and ravines which made excellent cover for the Japanese troops wanting to fight a defensive battle.

Allied code-breakers provided a lot of vital information at this time, and it helped the planners immensely to know what the Japanese were thinking. For a start, it became clear that reports as to the number of U.S. aircraft shot down and the number of ships sunk were being heavily exaggerated by the enemy. This made the Japanese commanders over-optimistic about their ability to fight off the Allies.

The first stages of the Leyte invasion began at first light on October 17, 1944, with mines being cleared and three small islands taken in the Leyte Gulf. Three days later a four-hour naval barrage preceded the landing of troops of the Sixth Army at 10.00am. The invading soldiers

USS Princeton (CVL 23) was lost in an air attack in the Sibuyan Sea during the Battle for Leyte Gulf.

did well in the face of determined resistance, and gradually took over most of the island. A major under-estimation of the enemy defensive plans by Allied commanders had allowed the Japanese to use their one remaining port to heavily reinforce their troops but, although this meant that the island was much harder to take than anticipated, the cost to the Japanese was immense. Their army had four divisions completely wiped out, and their navy lost 26 major warships, as well as 46 large merchant vessels. The Japanese air forces did little better, with more than half of their aircraft destroyed.

Dates:	October 20, 1944—U.S. landing on Leyte, Philippines October 23–26, 1944—Japanese battle fleet destroyed at Leyte Gulf
Participants:	Maj Gen Franklin C. Sibert's U.S. X Corps, including 1st Cavalry Division and 24th Infantry Division Maj Gen Hodge's U.S. XXIV Corps including the 7th and 96th Infantry Divisions U.S. Sixth Army, commanded by Lt Gen Walter Krueger 6th Ranger Infantry Battalion Sixth Army Service Command (ASCOM) under Maj Gen HJ. Casey U.S. Seventh Fleet, commanded by Vice Admiral Thomas C. Kinkaid Admiral William F. Halsey's Third Fleet Allied Air Forces commanded by Lt Gen George C. Kenney 16th Division of the Imperial Japanese Army under Lt Gen Shiro Makino Japanese Fourth Air Army and the Japanese First Air Fleet
Location of event:	Leyte, Philippines
Outcome:	The successful invasion of Leyte; The Japanese army lost four divisions and twenty-six major warships as well as more than half of their aircraft.

Troops of the 6th Panzer Army advance during the Battle of The Bulge.

DECEMBER 16–27, 1944

By the end of 1944, the Germans were in a desperate situation. The Red Army was advancing steadily from the east, and the Allies were at her borders in the west. More or less every night Allied bombers flew overhead and pounded just about every target they could find. In an attempt to defeat the Allies convincingly enough to force them into accepting a peace deal, Hitler tried one last massive counter-attack. This was mounted in the Ardennes, in what became known as the "Battle of the Bulge." He used all his reserve troops and what was left of the army's equipment, so it was clear that if the offensive failed, the war would effectively be over for Germany. The only issue in doubt would then be whether the Russians would take Germany first.

The Battle of the Bulge started on December 16, 1944, and continued until January 28, 1945. More than a million men took part, including around 600,000 Germans, 500,000 Americans, and 55,000 British troops. When the offensive first began, an SS armored column attacked an American unit and 7,500 men surrendered in the largest mass capitulation in United States history. The SS commander, Gruppenführer Joachim Peiper, ordered many of them to be executed, and when word got back to the rest of the American forces, the surrender rate went down dramatically.

The Allied commanders thought that it was a minor assault, but when Eisenhower finally realized that he had completely underestimated the situation, he sent the 101st Airborne to take the strategically important towns of Bastogne and Saint-Vith. Its fierce defense of Bastogne was to become a legendary action, and since bad weather prevented the Allied air forces from resupplying the airborne troops they had to hold out against enormous odds with few armored vehicles and little

Generals of the 101st Airborne division, review their positions at Bastogne.

food. Eventually, the weather cleared and Allied aircraft resupplied the beleaguered troops and attacked the Germans. They were finally relieved by Patton's 4th Armored Division on December 26, 1944.

By the time the battle was over, casualties were massive—on the Allied side 81,000 U.S. soldiers were injured and 19,000 killed, and British troops suffered 1,400 injured and 200 killed. The Germans' figure was 100,000 killed, wounded or captured, and a vast number of these "men" were only 15 or 16 years old.

Date:..........................December 16–27, 1944—The Battle of the Bulge
December 26, 1944—Patton relieves Bastogne.
Participants: .............U.S. 101st Airborne, VII Corps, Patton's Third Army and
General Hodges 2nd Armored Division
German forces under von Runstedt as Commander of the West
Field Marshal Model as tactical commander
Sixth SS Panzer Army under SS-Oberstgruppenführer Sepp Dietrich
Hasso von Manteuffel's Fifth Panzer Army
Brandenburger's Seventh Army
SS commander, Gruppenführer Joachim Peiper
Location of event:......The Ardennes
Outcome: ....81,000 U.S. soldiers were injured and 19,000 killed
1,400 British troops injured and 200 killed
100,000 Germans killed, wounded or captured

A Soviet Heavy Field Gun fires at German positions during the Battle for Budapest.

December 27, 1944

The Hungarians had been supporting the Germans throughout the war, but had lost thousands of troops in the abortive attempt to hold Stalingrad. As a result of this, they realized that Germany was going to be defeated, and sought to broker a peace deal with the Allies. Hitler was aware of this, and sent troops into Hungary on March 19, 1944 to prevent it falling into Allied hands. He installed a fanatically pro-German as prime minister—General Dome Sztojay had previously served as Hungarian minister to Berlin, and was well known to Hitler. General Sztojay ensured that Hungary continued to assist Germany in her war efforts, and also contributed to the large-scale deportation of Hungarian Jews.

Once the Red Army had forced the Romanians to surrender in August 1944, the Soviets regrouped and headed into Hungary on two separate fronts. One of these got bogged down whilst trying to take the town of Cluj, but the other, led by Marshal Malinovsky, broke through on 22 September, 1944. They continued to take ground, and on November 4 they reached the outskirts of Budapest. A second drive led by Marshal Tolbukhin performed a wide outflanking maneuver and by December 4 Hungary's capital city was completely encircled.

A determined defense of Budapest meant that it was able to hold out against the Red Army for some time. The city is divided into two parts, split by the River Danube—Pest, which is on the east bank, fell on 18 January 1945, and Buda, on the west bank finally fell after a fierce battle a month later, on 18 February. A Soviet-sponsored government was established, and this duly declared war on Germany on December 29, 1944.

Soviet Field Gun crew in the Streets of Budapest.

Date:........................December 27, 1944
Participants: ....Red Army under Marshal Malinovsky and Marshal
　　　　　　　　　　　　Tolbukhin
Location of event:......Budapest, Hungary
Outcome: ....The liberation of Hungary, the establishment of a Soviet-
　　　　　　　　　　　　sponsored government, and Hungary declaring war on
　　　　　　　　　　　　Germany

USS Pennsylvania and battleship of Colorado class followed by three cruisers move in line into Lingayen Gulf preceding the landing on Luzon.

Having successfully taken Leyte Island in October 1944, Allied forces in the Pacific had the stepping stone they needed to invade Luzon in the Philippines. General MacArthur wanted his forces to have access to airstrips that were closer than Leyte, however, and so he also ordered the invasion of the neighboring island of Mindoro. On December 12, 1944, U.S. troops landed on Mindoro and with the aid of precise intelligence information gathered by guerrillas, the invasion was a complete success, with no casualties on the American side. Within two weeks, there were two airfields in operation on the island, and this provided a major contribution to forthcoming operations.

The assault on Luzon began on January 9, 1945, when more than 2,500 landing craft descended on the beaches on the northern coast along the Lingayen Gulf. The Japanese had been fooled by extensive deception operations into thinking the attack was going to come from the south. These included extensive bombing raids and reconnaissance missions over targets in the south of the island, as well as increased guerrilla activity against Japanese communications lines. Mines were also cleared from the nearby coast to make it look as though the invasion was coming there.

The result of the deception was that the Japanese did indeed move many of their units to the south, which meant that American casualties were minimized. The improvements in command and communication also helped massive amounts of men and materials to be landed very quickly. The Japanese did their best to hold the Americans back, but they were unable to co-ordinate many of their manoeuvers, and gradually they

A line of Coast Guard landing barges, sweeping through the waters of Lingayen Gulf, carries the first wave of invaders to the beaches of Luzon, after a terrific naval bombardment of Jap shore positions.

were forced to relinquish their positions. By the end of May, most of the island was in Allied hands, and the planners could prepare for the next stage of the war.

Taking Luzon had a huge cost—the American forces took combat casualties of around 47,000, with some 10,380 killed and 36,550 wounded. Non-combat casualties were even higher at 93,400—this included 260 deaths; most of these were from disease. The Japanese meanwhile lost nearly all of the 230,000 military men they had on the island.

Date:.........................January 9, 1945
Participants: .............U.S. forces under General MacArthur's command, including:
Sixth Army under General Krueger
Eighth Army under General Eichelberger
11th Airborne and the 24th Division of the Eighth Army
1st Cavalry Division, under Maj Gen Verne D. Mudge
U.S. Seventh Fleet and an Australian Squadron under Admiral Kinkaid
U.S. Third Fleet under Admiral Halsey
U.S. Fifth and Thirteenth Air Force under the command of General Kenny
Japanese forces under General Tomoyuki Yamashita
Location of event:......Luzon, Philippines
Outcome: ....The successful invasion of the Philippines, at a cost of 10,380 Americans killed and 36,550 wounded; a further 93,400 became sick. Most of the 230,000 Japanese troops were killed or captured

Chow is served to American Infantrymen on their way to La Roche, Belgium.

JANUARY 16, 1945

As the American forces' defense of Bastogne drew to a close at the end of December 1944 in the Battle of the Bulge, they prepared for a counter-offensive—this was intended to strike out in a pincer movement to trap German units before they could withdraw from the region. The strike-back began two days before New Year, on December 29, 1944. The plan was for the U.S. Third Army to push north, while at the same time the U.S. First Army moved south. The intention was that they would meet at the village of Houffalize, and, in doing so, would encircle a long proportion of the German forces.

The push started out very slowly, with German units returning heavy fire. Things got worse when, on January 1, 1945, Hitler launched an operation he called "The Great Blow." This was intended to remove Allied air superiority, and most of the remaining Luftwaffe was thrown at Allied airbases in an intense bombardment. The attack did a great deal of damage, and within two hours 206 British and American aircraft had been destroyed. While this was a blow, the Allies were able to bring up replacements, whereas their German attackers no longer had the resources to do so. The Luftwaffe's total of 300 aircraft and 253 pilots lost signalled that this would be its last major offensive.

The massive losses incurred by the Luftwaffe meant that it was unable to provide much in the way of air support for the beleaguered German ground troops. By January 8, Hitler could see that both of his plans—the ground push through the Ardennes and the air offensive—were total failures. Consequently, he ordered his troops to withdraw, and by

Infantry Regiment advance into a Belgian town under the protection of a heavy tank.

January 16, the U.S. First and Third Armies reached their destination at Houffalize. Saint-Vith was recaptured on January 23, and on January 28 the Battle of the Bulge was officially declared over. For the Allies it had been expensive in both men and materials, but at this stage in the war they had lots of newly trained soldiers and vast quantities of supplies. For the Germans, however, it was a catastrophe—they lost most of their dwindling resources, and had very little left over to defend their homeland; defeat was only months away.

Date:..........................January 16, 1945
Participants:.............U.S. First and Third Armies
Location of event:......Houffalize, Belgium
Outcome:..................The Germans suffered a heavy defeat, losing much of their remaining men and equipment - consequently, this was their last major offensive of the war

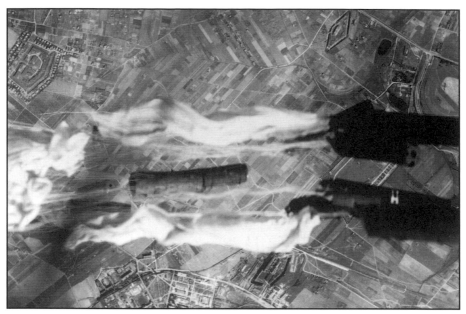

US Bombers drop weapons containers over Warsaw, the parachutes opening out in the slipstream.

JANUARY 17, 1945

In the spring of 1944, the Red Army continued to push the Axis front line back toward Germany. By mid-July, two major Soviet armies—the 1st Belorussian Front under Marshal Zhukov and the 1st Ukrainian Front under Marshal Vasilevski—began an assault that took them well into Poland. Within two weeks they had reached Warsaw, Poland's capital. However, they were ordered not to move into the city.

At that stage in the war the Poles had been under Nazi occupation for five years. They had, however, established two separate governments in exile—the largest and most powerful of which was in London. The other, a much smaller Communist group, was based in Moscow, and was very much under the influence of Stalin. A very well organized underground resistance movement had been built up in Warsaw—this was under the direct control of the London-based government. It had stockpiled large numbers of weapons—albeit that most of them were antiquated.

Stalin was paranoid about possible threats to his power, and he thought that the western-controlled Poles would be a major source of political trouble after the war was over. He therefore decided to encourage them to rise up against the German occupation army, under promises of Soviet assistance. When they did so, however, he deliberately ordered his forces to wait until the Nazis had annihilated all traces of the resistance movement.

This took 66 days, and by the end of this time the Germans had turned the entire might of their artillery and air forces in the region onto the beleaguered Polish freedom fighters. The ill-equipped Poles did not stand a chance without assistance from the Red Army, but this help never arrived. Fifty-five thousand Poles died as a result of Stalin's policy, and

German prisoners from a telephone exchange are marched to temporary captivity by their Polish captors.

German soldiers fire a salute over the graves of their comrades killed in Warsaw.

the Allies were appalled. In many ways, this was the start of the Cold War. Once the Germans had done his dirty work for him, Stalin moved the Red Army forward, and on January 17, 1945 the Soviets captured Warsaw.

Date: .... January 17, 1945
Participants: .... First Belorussian Front under Marshal Zhukov
First Ukrainian Front under Vasilevski
Location of event: ...... Warsaw, Poland
Outcome: .... The deaths of 55,000 Polish resistance fighters and civilians; the start of the Cold War

FEBRUARY 4–11, 1945.

By early 1945, the Soviets were poised to swoop down on Germany from the east and administer the final blow. The Allies had established themselves in much of western Europe, and were ready to enter Germany from the west across the open plains. In order to avoid the Allies and Soviets coming into conflict when they met, a conference was hastily organized to sort matters out in advance. This was held at Yalta between February 4 and 11, 1945. The major players were Franklin Roosevelt, Winston Churchill and Josef Stalin, although there were also many other participants.

The post-war reorganization of Europe was the main focus of the talks, and re-establishing the nations conquered by Germany was a central part of this. The Far East also came in for a lot of attention. Stalin agreed to come into the war against Japan within two or three months of the fall of Germany in return for a series of concessions. These included ensuring the stability of Outer Mongolia and the return of Southern Sakhalin and several adjacent islands, as well as joint Chinese-Russian operation of the Chinese Eastern and South Manchurian Railroads.

Conference of the Big Three at Yalta makes final plans for the defeat of Germany. Prime Minister Winston S. Churchill, President Franklin D. Roosevelt, and Premier Josef Stalin.

The Americans and British could not agree as to how Germany should be dealt with, but in the end it was decided that Germany would be divided into zones, each of which would be controlled by one of the three main parties—Britain, America and the Soviet Union. Russia would take responsibility for the eastern half of Germany, including Berlin. Stalin eventually agreed to allow France to become an occupier, too. The secret agreement also specified that Poland and Yugoslavia were to regain their independence. It was signed on February 11, 1945 by Roosevelt, Churchill, and Stalin.

Date: ....February 4–11, 1945
Participants: ....Franklin D. Roosevelt, Winston Churchill, and Josef Stalin
Location of event: ......Yalta, Crimea
Outcome: ....The organization of postwar Europe; Germany would be divided up between the Allies. Poland and Yugoslavia would also regain their independence. Stalin agreed to declare war on Japan after the fall of Germany in return for the return of Southern Sakhalin and other concessions

Planes of the US 8th Airforce over Germany.

FEBRUARY 13–14, 1945

Although Dresden was considered by many to be a target of low military significance, Winston Churchill described it as the "center of communications on Germany's eastern front." By early 1945, the Red Army was advancing en masse toward the city, and when the Allies attacked it on the night of February 13–14, 1945, they dropped 3,907 tons of bombs, reducing it to rubble. The damage was unparalleled— approximately 6 square miles (15sq km) were totally flattened, and 14,000 homes, along with large numbers of municipal buildings, destroyed.

The death toll was enormous—the exact figure will never be known for certain, but was particularly high since the city was temporarily housing a massive number of refugees who were fleeing from the advancing Soviets. Although it has been claimed that the destruction of Dresden was unnecessary, it was not only a major communications center but also a transportation hub, as well as a mass of munitions works, and so was of great strategic significance. Churchill also desperately wanted to demonstrate to the Russians just what the Allies were capable of doing to a city. It is possible that if Dresden had not been so convincingly destroyed, Stalin may not have stopped at Berlin, and the war may have escalated into a far worse conflict.

By this late stage in the war, life was getting harder for German civilians who lived in or near any of the towns and cities, especially those which had any kind of industrial capacity. More than 1,000 cities and towns were bombed by the Allies, during which nearly a million tons of

A traumatised German civilian makes her way throught the rubble of a German city, in the aftermath of the Allied airstrikes.

explosives were dropped. Most of the victims were women, children and the elderly, since those capable of fighting were away at one of the battle fronts. Although it was the Germans who pioneered the use of incendiary bombs, the Allies used them to create fire storms which destroyed the cities of Hamburg, Dresden, Cologne, Essen, Freiburg and Dortmund. These attacks also left large parts of Berlin and Munich in ruins. They also destroyed some 3.5 million homes and left 7.5 million Germans homeless. It is estimated that the Allied strategic bombing campaign killed between 750,000 and 1,000,000 civilians..

Date:........................February 13–14, 1945
Participants: ....RAF Bomber Command under Air Marshal Arthur Harris
Location of event:......Dresden, Eastern Germany
Outcome: ....The complete destruction of most of the city of Dresden. An unknown number of civilian deaths—possibly around 100,000

Marines of the 5th Division inch their way up a slope on Red Beach No. 1 toward Surbachi Yama as the smoke of the battle drifts about them.

February 19–March 16, 1944

Although Iwo Jima, at 8 square miles, was only a small island, its location offered the Allies the opportunity to stage bombing raids on mainland Japan using the B-29 Superfortress. It was therefore of key strategic importance. At the time that the Allied forces were preparing to invade in early 1945 there were already three airstrips on the island, and many of the Japanese air raids were being launched from them. Almost all the Kamikaze assaults originated from Iwo Jima, and so denying the Japanese the island as an operational base would mean that they would have to fly from Okinawa or Kyushu instead.

Before the invasion was launched, the island was subjected to 10 weeks of bombing by carrier-based aircraft and medium bombers—this was the heaviest of its kind in the war so far. For the three days before the landings took place there was also a large naval bombardment. The U.S. Marines had, in fact, asked for it to last 10 days but the request was turned down because there were insufficient ground-support ships, as they were still being used to take Luzon.

The invasion force went in at 9.00am on February 19, 1945, and under the cover of the naval bombardment were able to land relatively unopposed. When the naval protective barrage ended, however, the Japanese defenders came out of their bunkers and rained down sustained

Flag raising on Iwo Jima.

fire on the American forces. They were determined to make the Marines fight for every inch of land on the island, and their vast networks of interlinked caves, bunkers and pillboxes made clearing the defenders an enormously difficult task. The fighting continued until March 26, when the island was declared secure. The human cost of the 36-day offensive was staggering, with 6,821 U.S. troops killed and 19,217 wounded, and an estimated 20,000 Japanese soldiers killed, with just over 1,000 taken prisoner.

Date:...........................February 19–March 16, 1944
Participants: ....Admiral R. A. Spruance, Commander U.S. Fifth Fleet.
Vice Adm R. K. Turner as Joint Expeditionary Force
Commander
Lt Gen H. M. Smith, U.S. Marine Corps, as commander of
the Expeditionary Troops.
Location of event:......Iwo Jima
Outcome: ....6,821 U.S. troops were killed and 19,217 wounded. Around
20,000 Japanese soldiers were killed, and just over 1,000
taken prisoner

Hungarian troops watch Stukas pull out overhead.

March 6, 1945

After the Soviet attack on Hungary at the end of 1944 succeeded in taking Budapest, Hitler was furious that the city had fallen as it was a vital component in the defense of the oilfields located to the south of Lake Balaton. He therefore ordered the Sixth Panzer Army to retake the city in a strong counter-offensive aimed at pushing forward to the Danube and cutting off the spearhead of the Russian advance. This would stabilize the southeastern front and protect the vital oilfields.

The offensive was planned in great secrecy, and was named Operation "Frühlingserwachen" or Operation "Spring Awakening." Unfortunately for Hitler, however, the Sixth Panzer Army had been severely weakened by its previous activities and was incapable of sustaining a strong attack.

The offensive went ahead anyway, despite protests from the army commanders, and was launched on March 6, 1945. The Sixth Panzer Army led by Sepp Dietrich had support from various smaller Panzer divisions, although most were merely the remnants of the failed Ardennes offensive of winter 1944-45. The attack took the Russians by surprise and the Panzers made good gains in spite of having to move in bad weather and over marshy ground, in which many sank up to their turrets. The Soviets had thought the Germans to be all but finished, so the strength of their units shocked them. They soon recovered, however, and made a rapid counter-attack under the command of Marshal Tolbukhin. By March 17 they had succeeded in driving German forces back to where they started from. Hitler's offensive was doomed from the start, and the abortive mission collapsed, costing him large quantities of vital equipment. Sepp Dietrich, commander of the Sixth Panzer Army, commented that the unit was well named as they had only six tanks left. Anxious not to lose more of his precious armor, Hitler withdrew his tanks to defend Vienna.

German tank of the 6th Panzer army coming under attack

Date:	March 6, 1945
Participants:	German Sixth SS Panzer Army under SS-Oberstgruppenführer Sepp Dietrich and the 1st Cavalry Corps.
	Soviet forces under Marshal Tolbukhin
Location of event:	Lands in the region of the Danube
Outcome:	Sixth Panzer Army was reduced to six tanks; the Germans retreated badly beaten and this proved to be their last offensive in Hungary

MARCH 7, 1945

When the Allies began their push toward the center of Germany in early 1945, their biggest obstacle was the River Rhine—crossing this massive waterway without a bridge would be extremely difficult, and likely to cost them a lot of time as well as a huge number of casualties. When they took the remains of the city of Cologne on March 7, 1945, however, they found that, much to their surprise, the bridge at nearby Remagen was still standing. They launched an assault on it, during which time the enemy detonated explosive charges which had been laid in advance. Much to the Germans' frustration, however, these failed to trigger properly, and much of the bridge was left standing. They did their best to destroy it with sustained artillery barrages, but although much damage was done the bridge stayed up.

The Allies wasted no time in exploiting the opportunity, and under heavy fire poured huge numbers of troops and equipment over it. The weakened structure stood the immense amount of traffic for 10 days before collapsing, but by then the Allies had achieved their objective of establishing a bridgehead across the Rhine. Transport links with the

Allies race through Germany.

ancient town of Linz on the opposite bank were quickly re-established when a pontoon bridge became operational a mile or so downstream.

A further surprise was in store for the advancing Allied troops—even though the city of Cologne had been blasted into absolute ruins by Allied bombers, the inhabitants treated them as liberators rather than invaders. As the Reich's third largest city, this was a welcome, but unexpected outcome. The German population's deep seated fear of the Red Army meant that its joyous welcome for the Allied soldiers was due to its relief at not being subjected to the barbarous treatment it knew would be meted out by approaching Soviet soldiers.

Date:..........................March 7, 1945
Participants: .............U.S. 394th Regiment, 104th "Timberwolf" Infantry and 3rd "Spearhead" Armored Divisions
Location of event:......Cologne and Remagen
Outcome: ....The first crossing of the River Rhine by Allied troops

MARCH 9, 1945

Until the introduction of the B-29 Superfortress in 1944, the Japanese mainland was out of the range of land-based aircraft and it was only possible to use carrier-launched aircraft to bomb the enemy homeland. The drawback with this was that only small aircraft could take off from a carrier, and so the bomb loads were inherently light. The first air raid of this type on Japan had been the 1942 Doolittle Raid, which, while a major propaganda success, was insignificant militarily. The B-29, however, had a 1,500-mile range, and so the possibility of using it for strikes against Japan's industrial centers was discussed as soon as the first examples were delivered. The first time the aircraft was used against a Japanese target was when a number of them took off from China and bombed the Imperial Iron and Steel Works on the island of Kyushu on June 15, 1944. This, too, was not a success, and so when Pacific Island bases became available, the process of destroying Japanese war production centers was a top priority.

Although the destruction of factories was the main objective, because the vast majority of bombs dropped missed their targets by wide margins (often miles), a switch was made to the mass bombing of cities. Since many of Japan's buildings were wooden, it was felt that incendiary bombs should be tested, and so the first fire-bomb raid was made on the city of Kobe on February 3, 1945. This was a small success, and so plans were made for a much larger raid on Tokyo. The bomb-load was increased by

Damage after B-29 incendiary attack on Tokyo, Japan.

removing a lot of the armor-plating and several of the defensive weapons on each aircraft. This was possible due to the very poor quality of the Japanese defenses at night. The first incendiary raid on Tokyo took place on the night of February 23-24, 1945. In this operation 174 B-29s bombed the city, reducing around 1 square mile (3sq km) of it to ruins.

The strength of the raids was increased, and on the night of March 9-10 a massive raid by 334 B-29 Superfortresses hit Tokyo hard, dropping around 1,700 tons of incendiaries. The fires started generated so much heat that a fire-storm blew up, and around 16 square miles of the city were destroyed. It is thought that over 100,000 people died in the raid, the vast majority of whom were civilians. The bombing missions continued, and over the next few weeks large areas of many cities were flattened.

Date: .... March 9, 1945
Participants: .... General LeMay commanded the attack; 302 B-29s participated in the raid, with 279 arriving over the target
Location of event: ...... Tokyo
Outcome: .... 16 square miles of Tokyo destroyed and over 100,000 civilians killed. Fourteen B-29s were lost

The Burma campaign was fought by the Allies primarily for two reasons—to prevent the Japanese from invading India, and to keep the overland supply routes to China open. There were several aspects to this war that made it a very difficult theatre in which to operate. For a start, it was in a region where several different political agendas overlapped. On top of these problems there were the logistical ones caused by the extreme nature of the terrain, including rugged mountains, impenetrable forests and monsoon-drenched communications lines.

Whereas the Pacific campaign had clear objectives and made very good progress, the Burma campaign was dogged by conflicting interests and consequently became bogged down. When the conflict first started, it was thought that the vast armies the Chinese had at their disposal would play a significant role in fighting back against the Japanese. This turned out to be a forlorn hope, and was one of the greatest disappointments of the war. Instead of joining forces to attack the Japanese, most of the local warlords were more interested in fighting each other. After fighting an unproductive war for two years, the British appointed General Slim to take command of their forces in October 1943. Although the campaign itself saw some of the bloodiest conflicts of the entire war, under his brilliant leadership the army's performance improved considerably.

By early 1945, the British Fourteenth Army had begun to make good progress, consistently defeating the Japanese and moving across country in pursuit of them. By March they had left the jungles and were fighting on the open plains of Upper Burma. After a fierce battle, the 19th Indian Division liberated Mandalay on March 21, 1945. This was followed in early May by Operation "Dracula," which was an amphibious assault on Rangoon. The Japanese did not put up any resistance and the city was free once again.

Date: .... March 21, 1945
Participants: .... British Fourteenth Army under Field Marshal Sir William Slim and 19th Indian Division
Location of event: ...... Mandalay
Outcome: .... The Japanese were forced out of Burma, and the overland supply route to China was reopened
The Burma campaign was primarily fought for two reasons—to prevent the Japanese from invading India, and to keep the overland supply routes to China open.

U.S. Convoy which operates between Chen-Yi and Kweiyang, China, is ascending the famous twenty-one curves at Annan, China.

Transfer of wounded from USS Bunker Hill to USS Wilkes Barre, who were injured during fire aboard carrier following Japanese suicide dive bombing attack off Okinawa.

APRIL 1–JUNE 21, 1945

Okinawa, at around 480 square miles, is the largest island in the Ryukyus, and is surrounded by many other, smaller islands. It was of great strategic and political significance in the war in the Pacific. Located only 400 miles from Japan, Okinawa offered airbases that were much closer to the mainland than had previously been available. These, together with two deep-water ports, meant that the island could be used to launch an invasion of Japan itself. It was also in a key position with regard to many of Japan's most important communication routes. Considered by the Japanese to be home soil, the capture of Okinawa therefore offered the Allies a great propaganda victory as well as a major military asset.

Allied planners knew that Okinawa would be fanatically defended, and so the decision was made to take some of the smaller islands first. Since these were the site of several small naval bases, their capture would provide vital local support facilities, and make the logistics situation much simpler. This phase of the assault was mounted by soldiers from the U.S. Tenth Army under the command of Lieutenant General Simon B. Buckner, Jr on March 26, 1945.

When Allied forces launched the invasion of Okinawa—code-named Operation "Iceberg"—on April 1, 1945, it was the largest amphibious operation of the Pacific war, and the last major action before Japan surrendered. More than 1,300 ships were used, including over 40 aircraft carriers, 18 battleships, 200 destroyers and hundreds of other assorted

USS Bunker Hill burning after Japanese suicide attack.

vessels. Before the landing went ahead, the heaviest naval bombardment in history was mounted—over 3,800 tons of munitions were fired at the island in the first 24 hours alone. The initial invasion force of 60,000 American Marine and Army troops met with little opposition as they landed. However, the operation soon turned into the bloodiest conflict of the Pacific war. A total of 182,000 American soldiers were used in the action, and of these over 38,000 were wounded and 12,000 killed. The navy also took extremely heavy losses, with around 25 ships sunk and 165 others damaged—these were mostly caused by Kamikaze suicide planes. On the other side, over 107,000 Japanese and Okinawan troops were killed, as well as around 100,000 Okinawan civilians. More people died in the battle to take Okinawa than were killed by the atomic bombs dropped on Hiroshima and Nagasaki, and this certainly had an influence on the final decision to go ahead with the first-ever nuclear strike.

Date:	April 1–June 21, 1945
Participants:	U.S. Tenth Army under Lt. Gen Simon B. Buckner, Jr.
	More than 1,300 ships, including over 40 aircraft carriers, 18 battleships, 200 destroyers, and hundreds of other assorted vessels
	An invasion force of 60,000 American Marines and Army troops
Location of event:	Okinawa, Ryukyu Islands
Outcome:	Around 12,000 Americans were killed and 38,000 were wounded
	Over 107,000 Japanese and Okinawan troops were killed, as well as around 100,000 Okinawan civilians

Roosevelt's Funeral Procession on Pennsylvania Avenue, Washington DC.

April 12, 1945

In the early part of 1945, President Franklin D. Roosevelt's health was bad—it had been deteriorating for some time, and he finally died on the afternoon of April 12, 1945. Vice-President Harry Truman was immediately summoned to the White House by a 'phone call, and the first lady, Eleanor Roosevelt, gave him the bad news. He automatically assumed the mantle Roosevelt had worn for so long, and later that same evening, he was sworn in as the new President in a brief ceremony.

As a man who believed strongly in Roosevelt's war plans, Truman did his best to see them through. Shortly after becoming President, he was briefed about the new atomic weapon that was being developed, and was told that it should be completed within four months. Due to the gravity of the factors surrounding the use of such a weapon, Truman then approved the appointment of a committee to discuss the issues concerned. The committee came to the conclusion that the Japanese Emperor and his military advisors had to be shocked into agreeing to an unconditional surrender. It was also felt that if this was done carefully, it would save an enormous number of lives on both sides. While these decisions were being made, American troops were being slaughtered in the battle for Okinawa on an unprecedented scale, and the idea of taking similar losses whilst trying to invade the Japanese mainland was unthinkable. In the committee's eyes, a solution had to be found, and the atomic bomb seemed to be the answer.

President Harry S. Truman.

The Germans surrendered 25 days after Truman took office, and so he was able to spend more time on the matter of concluding the war in the Pacific. When the news came that the test of the atomic bomb had been successful, he was faced with what was probably the biggest decision of the century. Should he use the bomb or not? In the end, he felt that the idea of sending hundreds of thousands more American troops to their deaths in an invasion of Japan was too great a price to pay. He knew that the Japanese people would not surrender, and that unless he was prepared to kill most of the civilian population, a land war could not be won. He therefore gave the order to drop the atomic bomb on Hiroshima, and act that he has been vilified for to this day.

Date:.........................April 12, 1945
Participants: ....Harry Truman and Franklin D. Roosevelt
Location of event:......The White House
Outcome: ....Vice-President Truman became President

Soviet soldiers storm Berlins Reichstag building.

APRIL 21, 1945

Toward the end of the war, the massive increase in the output of the Russian war machine meant that the Red Army was able to go into battle with all the armor it could possibly need. Consequently, the Germans had been beaten back on every front in the east, and by January 1945 the Soviets were in a confident mood. They had wrapped up most of the Axis forces in southeastern Europe, and had assembled sufficient manpower to deal with any last-minute stands by their opponents. They had also amassed a vast army in eastern Poland and on January 12 they pushed forward through central Poland and onto German soil. As the Red Army progressed, German authorities became ever more oppressive in their attempts to maintain control over their population. Anyone who questioned the "final victory" of their country, or was caught listening to foreign news on the radio, was executed.

In the closing stages of the war, when Hitler realized that defeat was certain, he decided that all Germany should be destroyed in the classic "scorched earth" manner as a last act of defiance. He felt that it was what the German people deserved for allowing themselves to be beaten. In March 1945 he sent the order for the destruction of Germany's stores of food, clothing and military equipment, power stations, electrical distribution systems, and all communications centers and transport facilities. Likewise, every factory was to be razed to the ground to stop it falling into the hands of the Allies. On March 30 the Red Army crossed into Austria and captured Vienna on April 13. Soon afterward soldiers from the U.S. 69th Infantry Division met up with troops from the Russian 58th Guards Division at the River Elbe—this effectively cut northern Germany from the south. Berlin was now within the grasp of the Soviets, and a massive assault was launched by the Red Army on April 16 to take Germany's capital city. The Soviets reached Berlin on April 21.

Soviet tank soldier dancing to celebrate victory in Berlin.

Date:..........................April 21, 1945
Participants: ....The Red Army under Field Marshals Georgi Zukhov and
                          Ivan Koniev
                          The German Army Group "Vistula," comprising:
                          von Manteuffel's Third Panzer Army to defend Berlin's north
                          General Theodor Busse's Ninth Army to defend Berlin's east
                          Field Marshal Ferdinand Schörner to defend Berlin's south
                          and west
Location of event:......The outskirts of Berlin
Outcome: ....Herman Göring—Hitler's legal successor—and Chief of
                          General Staff Heinz Guderian were both dismissed by Hitler
                          after asking for surrender

To a society that was instilled with Nazism, the fall of the Third Reich had a devastating effect—particularly the youngest soldiers such as these Hitlerjugend, here seen being decorated by Hitler on one of his last public engagements.

APRIL 30–MAY 7, 1945

When the Red Army reached Berlin on April 21, 1945, the entrenched German troops did their best to defend the city with a ruthless fanaticism. This was not only to uphold the pride of the nation, but also to give their refugee civilian population the time to escape toward the safety of the west and away from the clutches of the barbaric Soviet soldiers. Their stand against an overwhelming superior force lasted only 12 days—an incredible feat given the tremendous lack of supplies and equipment.

Hitler decided to remain in Berlin, and when the entire city was encircled by the Red Army, he ordered his Twelfth and Ninth Armies to break through to relieve them on April 20. Neither army was able to break through the enemy's defenses, however, and Hitler's much-needed relief never came. In the meantime, an enormous battle was being waged in the streets as house-to-house combat ensued.

On April 30, Adolf Hitler married his mistress Eva Braun, whom he felt had been the only person who had remained loyal to him throughout the war. Then, knowing that the end had come, Hitler committed suicide. Three days later, on 2 May 1945, the "Thousand Year" Reich came to an end as the remnants of the German government surrendered. The last days of fighting in Berlin had been some of the most intense of the entire war. The Red Army lost around 305,000 killed, and the Germans as many as 325,000, including civilians.

Hitler and Eva Braun married on 29th April 1945, the following day, she commited suicide by swallowing poison two minutes before Hitler took his own life.

On May 4 the German High Command surrendered all its forces in northwest Germany, Holland and Denmark to Field Marshal Montgomery. Three days later, at General Eisenhower's headquarters in Rheims, Admiral Friedeburg and General Jodl officially signed Germany's unconditional surrender to the Allies. Fighting stopped at 12am on the morning of May 9, and across Europe the guns were silenced.

Dates: .... April 30, 1945—Adolf Hitler commits suicide
May 7th, 1945—Unconditional surrender of all German forces to the Allies
Participants: .... Adolf Hitler, his mistress Eva Braun and Dr Joseph Goebbels, with his wife and six children.
Location of event: ...... The Führerbunker in the gardens of the Reich Chancellery in Berlin
Outcome: .... Admiral Friedburg and General Jodl officially signed Germany's unconditional surrender to the Allies; the end of the war in Europe

LSM-151 was part of a US Naval Force assisting the Australian Army during the landing.

JUNE 10, 1945

As the Pacific war progressed, the Americans focused on invading islands that would lead them to an invasion of the Japanese mainland in the shortest possible time. In the meantime, the Australians, backed by large numbers of Dutch and other Allied troops, concentrated on cutting the Japanese off from the resources they needed to keep the war going. Since Borneo was a major source of vital commodities—especially oil—it was a priority target.

The Australians not only ensured that they used sufficient pre-assault bombardments but that they had overwhelming numbers of troops in their invasions during the Borneo campaign. This tactic more or less assured victory, and kept casualties to a minimum. In the first phase, at the battle for the neighboring island of Tarakan on May 1, the Australian troops outnumbered the Japanese by about six times. In the second phase, for Brunei, this figure was around nine times, and in the third and final phase there were around eight times as many Australians as Japanese.

Planning for the invasion of Borneo started in April 1945, but preliminary bombardments on Balikpapan did not start until June 10. This was an important oil port, with pre-war annual exports amounting to some 1.8 million tons of fuel oil and petroleum products a year. It was therefore of immense importance to the Japanese war machine, and consequently very heavily defended.

The Australian planners did their best to ensure that their troops had the best possible chance of landing unharmed. As a result, 20 days before troop landings began, key defensive positions were pounded by bombers and naval gunships. In the last 15 days alone, over 23,000 shells were fired, and each day the best part of 200 B-24 Liberator bombers dropped ordinance on the coastal defenses.

The success of the bombardments is demonstrated by the casualty figures—on the first day of landings on June 10 only three Australian soldiers were killed. The Japanese fought fiercely, but were beaten back by superior numbers of well-trained troops. Within nine days of the invasion, the Balikpapan area had been secured, with a total cost of 229 Australian dead as compared to an estimated 2,000 Japanese.

There is still heated debate about whether it was worth risking the lives of so many Australians when the end of the war was so close. At the time, however, only a select few knew about the atomic bomb, and without it the war could easily have lasted another year. Cutting off Japanese oil supplies in this scenario was therefore an important contribution toward ending the war.

Date:	June 10, 1945
Participants:	18th, 21st, and 25th Brigades of the Australian 7th Division, under Maj Gen E. J. Milford
	Large numbers of Liberator bombers
	A large naval bombardment force
	Minesweepers and American Naval diving teams helped clear the sea of mines and underwater obstacles
Location of event:	Borneo
Outcome:	The Allied liberation of Borneo, and the cessation of a large proportion of the oil supplies as well as many other vital resources needed by the Japanese war machine

*1940's -- Roswell army air field, New Mexico -- Col. Paul Tibbetts, Jr., of Miami, Fla.,
poses in front of his B-29 Superfortress "The Enola Gay" (named for his mother). The Enola
Gay is the same plane he piloted when his bombardier dropped the first atom bomb over
Hiroshima, Japan.*

AUGUST 6, 1945

In the summer of 1945 the Allies were faced with a long and bitter
battle to defeat the Japanese. An intelligence report was presented to
President Truman on June 30 which stated that the Japanese believed
"that unconditional surrender would be the equivalent of national
extinction." It was, therefore, going to take an extraordinary event
to persuade the Emperor to accept a solution that would be seen as a
disgrace to the country. Recent events, such as the invasions of Iwo Jima
and Okinawa, had shown that the Japanese would fight to the very last
drop of blood for every inch of ground. An invasion of their homeland
would doubtless be fought against with a similar ferocity.

Truman, therefore, listened carefully to his senior advisors, especially
the Secretary of War. One of the arguments made for use of the bomb
was that the Soviets were threatening to expand throughout Europe.
They had already taken Romania, Bulgaria, Yugoslavia, Czechoslovakia
and Hungary, and it was felt that they might well continue west and
complete what Hitler had failed to do. A demonstration of America's
ability to deliver a nuclear weapon would be likely to rein Stalin in and
prevent the start of a whole new war.

The Russians had already declared their plans to attack Japan in
late August to the Allies, and this confirmed their fears that the Soviets
intended to seek world domination. With the first test of the new bomb
successfully performed at Alamogordo, New Mexico, on July 16, the time
had come to make a decision. After further discussions, Truman—with
Churchill's consent and the agreement of his chief advisors—ordered the
dropping of the first atomic bomb on Hiroshima.

At the time this photo was made, smoke billowed 20,000 feet above Hiroshima while smoke from the burst of the first atomic bomb had spread over 10,000 feet on the target at the base of the rising column. August 5, 1945. Two planes of the 509th Composite Group, part of the 313th Wing of the 20th Air Force, participated in this mission; one to carry the bomb, and the other to act as escort.

The bomb, known as Little Boy, was delivered by a B-29 called Enola Gay which took off from the airbase at Tinian at 2.45am on August 6, 1945. It flew for six and a half hours, and dropped its load at exactly 8:16am over the city of Hiroshima on the Japanese mainland. It had the equivalent power of 20,000 tons of TNT; it detonated at 2,000 feet, and seconds later everything within 4 square miles was obliterated. It is estimated that around 80,000 civilians died instantly, and a similar number died later as a result of radiation sickness. The Japanese were then warned that if they did not surrender they could expect "a rain of ruin from the air, the like of which had never been seen on this earth."

Date:........................August 6, 1945
Participants: ....The bomb, Little Boy, was dropped by a B-29 called Enola Gay
Location of event:......Hiroshima, Japan
Outcome: ....The deaths of around 160,000 people, and the first steps towards Japanese acceptance of surrender

When the Allies were trying to work out how to end the Pacific war, it was agreed that it would be necessary to drive the Japanese off the mainland of Asia. The Japanese had large armies in Manchuria, which bordered the Soviet Union. If the Soviets could be brought into the conflict, they would be able to make an enormous contribution to the war effort by attacking the Japanese armies based there. This would open up another front which the Japanese, who were already resource-starved, could ill-afford to defend. At the Yalta and Potsdam conferences in 1945, Stalin agreed to join the war once matters in Europe had been concluded.

On August 8, 1945, two days after the atomic bomb was dropped on Hiroshima, the Soviets declared war on Japan and invaded Manchuria. They assembled around 1,500,000 troops for the offensive, split over three army groups—these were the 1st and 2nd Far East Fronts, and the Transbaikal Front. In total, they were equipped with 5,500 tanks and 26,000 artillery pieces and supported by 3,900 aircraft. Facing them was a Japanese force of around 1,000,000 men from the poorly equipped Kwantung Army, who had no armor, tanks or aircraft to back them up.

The entry of the Soviet Union into the Pacific theatre caused havoc in the Japanese government, and Emperor Hirohito called the Supreme Council together to try to get the military commanders to accept the proposed surrender. He could not get an agreement from them, and the discussion stalled. The next day, August 9, 1945, a second atomic bomb was dropped—this time the hapless target was the city of Nagasaki. Emperor Hirohito was appalled, and, with government consent, he and Prime Minister Suzuki sought an immediate peace with the Allies.

Date:..........................August 8, 1945
Participants: ....The Soviet First and Second Far East Fronts and the Transbaikal Front with around 1,500,000 troops and heavy armour, artillery and aircraft
The lightly-armed Japanese Kwantung Army with around 1,000,000 troops
Location of event:......Manchuria (also known as Manchuko)
Outcome: ....The Japanese were quickly overrun by the Soviets. The threat of an invasion of Japan itself helped influence the decision to surrender

Joseph Stalin.

With the dropping of the first atomic bomb on Hiroshima on August 6, 1945, the Japanese Emperor Hirohito was shocked, but unable to persuade his government to accept Allied surrender terms. Two days later, the Soviets declared war on Japan and invaded Manchuria—even this, though, did not convince Japanese military commanders to change their minds.

The American and British governments were desperate to force the Japanese to accept surrender terms before the Soviet Union invaded their country. It was almost certain that if Stalin occupied Japan, he would never agree to relinquish it, and this would most likely result in another world war. When the first bomb was dropped, arrangements were already in place for a second atomic detonation. This was scheduled to be dropped on the town of Kokura, and a B-29 named Bock's Car took off from Tinian at 3.49am on the morning of August 9, 1945 to deliver the bomb known as Fat Man. When the aircraft arrived over Kokura, clouds obscured it from view, and so the bomb was released over the secondary target of Nagasaki. It exploded at just after 11.00am at a height of about 1,650 feet above the small coastal port. Fat Man had the equivalent power of 22,000 tons of TNT, and it flattened everything within 3 square miles. A column of smoke rose 60,000 feet into the air, and about 150,000 people died either on the scene or within the year. The nature of the terrain around Nagasaki saved many thousands more from being killed or injured, as the low hills reduced the blast considerably.

The dropping of the second atomic bomb demonstrated to all concerned that America had the power to literally destroy Japan, and Emperor Hirohito was finally able to get his government to agree to a peace deal.

Date: ....August 9, 1945
Participants: ....The bomb, Fat Man, was dropped from a B-29 named Bock's Car flown by Major Sweeney.
Location of event: ......Nagasaki, Japan
Outcome: ....The deaths of 150,000 people within the year

*Smoke billows up over Nagasaki, Japan after bombing by atomic bomb on 9 August 1945.
Two planes of the 509th Composite Group, part of the 313th Wing of the 20th Air Force,
participated in this mission; one to carry the bomb, the other to act as escort.*

World War II ends when representatives of Japan and the Allied Forces meet and Japan signs the instruments of surrender aboard the battleship USS Missouri (BB 63) in Tokyo Bay.

AUGUST 14–SEPTEMBER 2, 1945

When the second atomic bomb was dropped at Nagasaki on August 9, 1945, the Japanese Emperor Hirohito finally managed to get his government to accept the unacceptable, and the next day they agreed to seek an unconditional surrender. The details took many days to sort out, and in the meantime American bombing raids continued—these reached a peak on August 14, when 804 B-29s hit Tokyo.

On August 15 Emperor Hirohito made a radio broadcast to the nation telling them of Japan's surrender. At this point the Allies ceased all further military actions, and instead mounted an enormous relief campaign to deliver aid to the thousands of Allied prisoners of war held in Japan, China, Manchuria and Korea. Well over a thousand B-29s took part in 900 missions to 154 camps. These delivered food and clothing to around 63,500 prisoners, many of whom were in the last stages of starvation; in all, 4,470 tons of supplies were delivered.

General Douglas MacArthur was quickly appointed to command the occupation forces in Japan, and on August 29 American troops landed near Tokyo and began the formal occupation. The next day the British reoccupied Hong Kong, and preparations were made on board the USS Missouri, which was anchored in Tokyo Bay, for the surrender ceremony. This took place on September 2 1945, and President Harry Truman officially proclaimed "Victory in Japan" Day, known as "VJ Day." The next few days saw big changes in the region.

F4U's and F6F's fly in formation during surrender ceremonies; Tokyo, Japan. USS Missouri left foreground.

On September 3, General Yamashita, who was the Japanese commander of the Philippines, surrendered to General Wainwright at Baguio. This was followed on September 4 by the capitulation of Japanese troops on Wake Island. General MacArthur entered Tokyo on September 8, the next day Japanese forces in Korea surrendered, those in Burma did likewise on September 13.

Dates:	August 14, 1945—Japanese agree to unconditional surrender; Emperor Hirohito's radio announcement of surrender
	September 2, 1945—Japanese sign the surrender agreement; V-J Day
Participants:	Emperor Hirohito announced the surrender
	General Douglas MacArthur signed it as Supreme Allied Commander
	Foreign Minister Mamoru Shigemitsu signed on behalf of the Japanese Government, and General Yoshijiro Umezu on behalf of the Japanese Imperial General Headquarters
	Admiral Chester Nimitz of the U.S. Navy
	Hsu Yung-Ch'ang of the Republic Of China
	Bruce Fraser of the U.K.
	Kuzma Derevyanko of the Soviet Union
	Thomas Blamey of Australia
	L. Moore Cosgrave of Canada
	General Jacques Leclerc of France
	C.E.L. Helfrich of the Netherlands
	Leonard M. Isitt of New Zealand.
	General Yamashita later surrendered the Japanese army in the Philippines to General Wainwright at Baguio
Location of event:	The ceremony was held on board the U.S.S. Missouri, in Toko Bay.
Outcome:	The end of World War II

Nuremberg Trials: looking down on the defendants' dock.

NOVEMBER 20, 1945

When Germany surrendered on May 7, 1945, the Nazi rule of terror in Europe was over, and efforts to re-establish the rule of law began. Whilst this process started on the ground more or less straight away, bringing the Nazi leaders to trial took more than six months. Before it could go ahead, the Allies first had to agree on how the prosecutions should be conducted. There were calls, for instance, for Nazi leaders to be shot on capture and for Germany's industrial centers to be dismantled and the country turned into an agricultural society.

In the end it was agreed that a legal prosecution should go ahead, although arguments over where it should be held raged back and forth. The Soviets wanted it to be in Berlin on what was now their soil. However, the other Allies managed to persuade them that the Palace of Justice in Nuremberg was a better choice.

In early May 1945, President Truman appointed Robert Jackson, the Supreme Court Justice, as the chief U.S. counsel for the prosecution of Nazi war criminals. Then, in late May, Heinrich Himmler, who had been Hitler's most powerful and terrifying Nazi leader, committed suicide rather than face prosecution. Preparations for the Nuremberg trials continued, and on August 8, 1945, an agreement was signed to establish the legal frameworks under which the process of law could go ahead. The British representative Sir Geoffrey Lawrence was elected President of the International Military Tribunal on October 14, and on October 19 indictments were issued against the major defendants. The prosecution of Hitler's henchmen started at 10am on November 20, 1945, although by this time Robert Ley, the former chief of the German Labor Front, had already committed suicide.

The trial itself was a long, drawn-out affair that pored over events in enormous detail. Gruesome evidence was displayed, and some of the Nazi perpetrators were visibly shocked at what they saw. Some witnesses, such as Field Marshal Friedrich Paulus, provided testimony that incriminated other defendants, whereas others, such as Göring, gave robust rebuttals of charges made against them.

The verdicts were handed down on October 1, 1946, and 11 of the 21 defendants were sentenced to death. One of those was Göring, but before the execution could be carried out, he committed suicide by swallowing a cyanide pill. On October 16, 1946, the other 10 were hanged in Nuremberg. Subsequent tribunals were then held to prosecute others accused of Nazi war crimes—these included 23 Nazi physicians and 20 members of the Einsatzgruppen death squads. Seven of the former and 14 of the latter defendants were sentenced to death. The tribunals then went on to prosecute Nazi ministers, judges and other officials. The whole process ended on April 13, 1949, taking an overall total of four years to complete.

Date:.......................November 20, 1945
Participants: ....Supreme Court Justice Robert Jackson as chief U.S. counsel
Sir Geoffrey Lawrence as President of the International Military Tribunal
All the leading members of the Nazi party who had been captured.
Location of event:......Nuremberg
Outcome: ....Of the leading Nazis, several, including Heinrich Himmler, Herman Göring, and Robert Ley committed suicide. Of the remaining 20 prosecuted in the first trial, 11 were executed by hanging. Later trials included prosecutions of Einsatzgruppen death squad members, concentration camp physicians and others who played a part in Hitler's tyranny